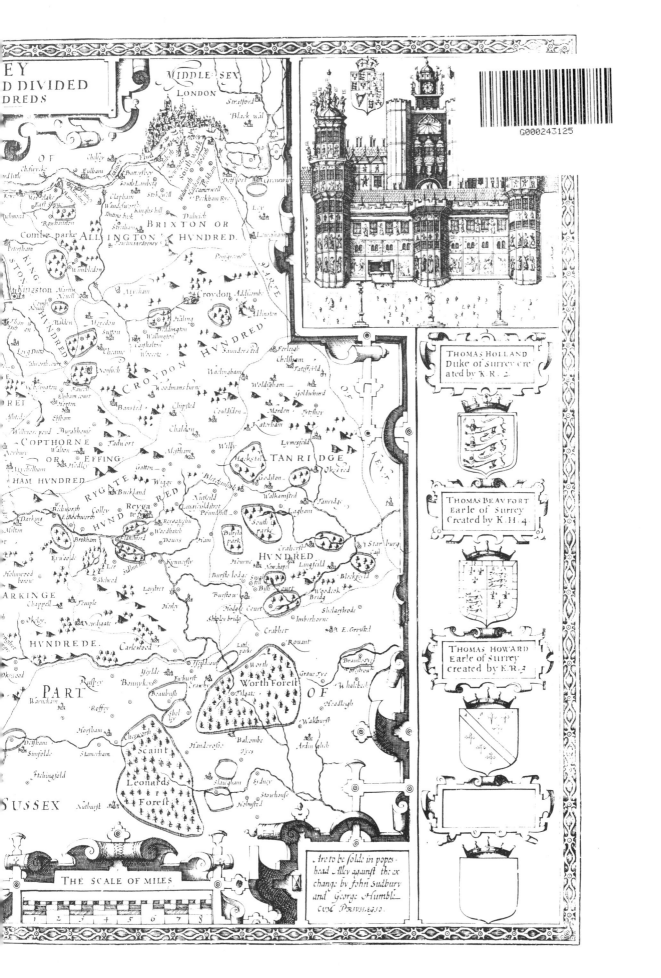

# THE BOOK OF COBHAM

FRONT COVER: Cobham Mill from *Rambles By Rivers* published in 1844.
The author of this book, James Thorne, described Cobham as 'quite a
model of a sequestered country hamlet'.

Church Stile House and lychgate from a drawing by Alan Parkinson.

# THE BOOK OF COBHAM

BY

## DAVID C. TAYLOR

'The Earth is the Lord's and the Fulness Thereof' — *Psalm 24*

BARON
MCMXCV

PUBLISHED IN THE BARRACUDA COLLECTION IN 1982,
REVISED EDITION 1987
FOURTH IMPRESSION IN 1995 BY BARON BIRCH FOR QUOTES LIMITED
PRODUCED BY KEY COMPOSITION, HILLMAN PRINTERS (FROME) LIMITED,
CHENEY & SONS LIMITED AND WBC BOOKBINDERS

ISBN 0 86023 171 2

*Addendum page 110 paragraph three, line one*
*For 1826 read 1843.*

# Contents

# Acknowledgements

A book of this sort can never be the work of one man alone, and I am conscious of the labours of other historians of far greater experience than my own, and of the debt that I owe to them and to the many other local people who have assisted my own researches over the years. I wish to acknowledge a particular debt of gratitude to T. E. C. Walker FSA whose knowledge, research and writings must be the groundwork for anyone involved in a study of Cobham's history. Conway Walker's friendship has been a tremendous encouragement and support and I am grateful to him for the many hours we have spent discussing local history and for his help in the preparation of this book. I should also like to thank the many friends who have encouraged me in the preparation of this book and my wife, Carrie, for her enthusiasm and patience.

The Hassell illustrations of Cobham and the Porden drawings of Cobham Park appear by permission of the Trustees of the British Museum as does the Gilray cartoon. The portrait of Ligonier appears by permission of the National Army Museum. I am grateful to the Tate Gallery for permission to reproduce the portrait of Mrs Vernon Lushington and to the National Portrait Gallery for permission to reproduce the pictures of Matthew Arnold, Mrs Ward, Spencer Stanhope, Fairfax, and Lloyd George. The *Surrey Comet* has allowed me to reproduce the photograph of Downside Bridge during the 1968 floods and the Surrey Archaeological Society has kindly allowed the reproduction of a number of maps, sketches and other illustrations from the Society's collections. I am also grateful to the Surrey Record Office at Kingston and Guildford for permission to reproduce material in its care. The map of the Mole terraces from Millward and Robinson's *Landscapes of Britain: Thames and The Weald* is reproduced by permission of Macmillan, London and Basingstoke and the stills from 'Winstanley' by permission of Kevin Brownlow and Andrew Mollo/BFI Production Board. The Science Museum have kindly provided copies of 'The Red Rover' and 'A Scene on the Portsmouth Road' from C. G. Harper's *The Portsmouth Road*. Extracts from the journals of A. J. Munby are by permission of Trinity College Library, Cambridge, and the copy of the Chertsey Abbey Charter (Cotton Vit. A xiii f.38 v) was from *The History of Effingham* and is reproduced by permission of the British Library. The Crawter map of Painshill is reproduced by permission of the Trustees of the Will of the late Major Peter George Evelyn. The portrait of Charles Hamilton appears by kind permission of Lady Tessa Agnew and the sketch of Ham Manor is reproduced by kind permission of John L. Baker.

In the following list I hope that I have included all those who have lent photographs and objects or given information and advice: Mrs A. M. Arbury; the Automobile Association; R. Baker; B. Bernstrom; Mrs B. Bore; L. Bowerman; Miss B. M. Bradnack; Miss J. Bronkhurst; G. Brown; P. Chew; the Misses Christmas; Cobham Park Estate; C. Combe; Countess Franzero; Mrs M. Higgins; House of Lords Records Office; L. Ingold; N. Kitz OBE; Mrs A. Lansdell and the staff of Weybridge Museum; Metropolitan Police Office; C. Norris; Miss V. Pike; Shoosmith and Lee; Rev J. Smith (Parish Magazines and Vestry Minutes); B. Symonds; Mrs J. Wagstaff; T. E. C. Walker; Councillor L. B. Yates, J. S. Clark and A. Parkinson.

Finally I am most grateful to Ian Greig, editor of the *Cobham Parish Magazine* and to all those who deliver the magazine, thereby assisting in the distribution of publicity for this book. I must also thank J. Farmer; C. Worsfold; Messrs Trenchard and Arlidge; Mrs M. Judd and the staff of Bookmark; Mrs Bamber and the staff of Cobham Library; the Cobham Conservation Group; the Cobham Gardening Club; the Cobham Residents Association; Messrs Dawson Strange for help with photographic work; and all Cobham traders and residents who have helped in the promotion of *The Book of Cobham*.

I apologise for any errors or omissions of fact or attribution which may have occurred.

# Foreword

## by Pamela A. Church, Mayor of Elmbridge

An interesting facet of local history is the way in which our communities, whether boroughs, towns or villages, develop. Elmbridge itself has existed as a borough only since the local government reorganisation of 1974, being formed from the two urban districts of Walton and Weybridge and Esher. Esher UDC originally included Cobham amongst its other villages. Cobham itself, rather like Gaul, was once divided into three parts, Street Cobham, Church Cobham and Tilt Cobham.

It is this sense of historical evolution that gives Cobham its essence as a community, and this history, demonstrated all about us, makes Cobham such an interesting and attractive place not only for its inhabitants but also for new-comers and for visitors. To me, as a relatively new resident, this sense of history is revealed in buildings old and new like the mill and the Old Bear, in features like Painshill Park, famous for the landscape created by Charles Hamilton and its connections with the East India Company through the architect Richard Jupp, and in the beauty of the cherry trees on the Tilt, planted as a memorial to the dead of World War II.

But there is so much more to Cobham as readers of David Taylor's book will soon understand, whether they be life-long residents, newcomers or visitors. It is the fascination and importance of this book that it reveals much that has been forgotten, reminds us of the centuries over which our beautiful village has developed, and prompts us all to ensure that Cobham remains attractive to its residents, present and future, and to its visitors.

*Pamela Church*

# Introduction

The town of Cobham is not one of this country's historic showpieces, neither does it contain much to distinguish it from any other similar sized community. However it does have a long and varied history which makes it different from any other place and which gives it an identity of its own.

The ease and speed with which we can now travel, linked with today's instant and disposable society, have only accentuated our basic need for roots and a sense of permanency in our surroundings.

Through the wholesale destruction of much of the individual character of our towns and cities over the past few decades, we have become painfully aware of our need for buildings, landscapes and communities with which we can identify and where we can feel at home. This has been underlined by the meteoric increase in genealogical research and interest in local history. Civic and conservation societies are stronger today than ever before, as we become aware of our surroundings and the need to preserve the best of the past and replace the old and worn out using the best of modern day skills and craftsmanship.

The history of Cobham cannot be contained in a book of this size, or indeed, in any book. This can only be a pot-pourri to whet the reader's appetite and stimulate interest. I hope that through this book you will see something of the continuity of history in Cobham, and that you will have a deeper appreciation of the community, not only for what it has been in the past, but also for what it can be in the future.

# Dedication

For Carrie, Nicholas and Andrew

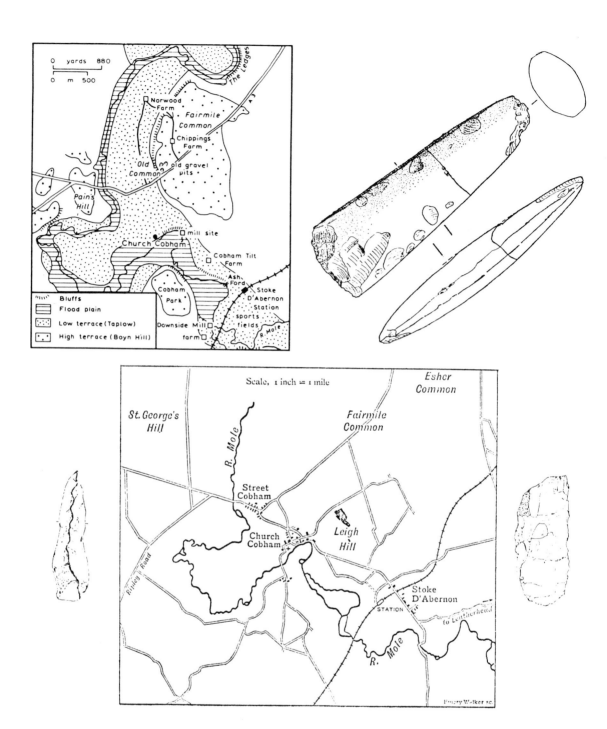

ABOVE LEFT: The terraces of the River Mole around Cobham; RIGHT: polished flint axe found near Norwood Farm in 1968 (one third actual size) and BELOW LEFT & RIGHT: Mesolithic flint axe found in the River Mole in 1965; CENTRE: the environs of Cobham, showing the site of the Iron Age and later settlements on Leigh Hill.

# *Early Days*

The names of many of our cities, towns and villages often provide a clue to both the early history of the place and the reason for its geographical position. Cobham is no exception. Until as late as the eighteenth century, Cobham was often called by its former name of Coveham or Covenham — a name first recorded in the seventh century.

The origin of the name seems to be found in the settlement's position in a large distinctive bend of the river Mole. *Cove* and *ham* are the component parts of the name, cove being the curve of the river and ham being a common suffix indicating someone's home. Because *ham* is frequently used in conjunction with a personal name, it has also been suggested that Cobham was Cofa's Ham, but this seems unlikely.

Cobham is now regarded as a single entity comprising Street Cobham, Church Cobham and Tilt Cobham, which were all separate communities at one time, Street Cobham and Church Cobham being joined by the road aptly named Between Streets. It is now one of the largest parishes in Surrey covering some 5,300 acres and with a current population nearing 10,000.

From a geographical viewpoint, Cobham covers an area of low relief. In the northwest, the Mole flows at a level below 50 feet and only a small area of Oxshott Heath reaches a height of 225 feet.

While the course of the Mole has been a crucial factor in the siting of Cobham, the river's terraces, or levels, which are particularly evident in the area, have been just as important in the siting of individual buildings.

There is no shortage of surface water passing through the parish from the Mole's large catchment area in Surrey and Sussex, and this accounts for the sometimes heavy seasonal flooding. The flood plain is at its widest south of the river, and this was clearly seen in the severe flooding of 1968, when most of the open land on that side of the river became an enormous lake.

The edge of the Lower Terrace is prominent around Cobham Tilt and by the Mill. The wisdom of our ancestors is clearly demonstrated in the siting of some of Cobham's oldest properties, such as Cedar House, Mill Cottage ,Ham Manor and the parish church which, despite their close proximity to the river, have largely remained unaffected by flooding.

The Higher Terrace, which is the oldest, is marked by the more ancient habitable sites of Cobham Park, Painshill and the Fairmile. These upper terraces, being older, have been subjected to plenty of erosion and so the proportion of sand and gravel is higher here. The gravel deposits of the Fairmile Common were much in demand for road making and large pits were opened up close to the Portsmouth Road. Although most have long since been abandoned, the hummocky disturbed ground is still much in evidence. In 1822, Joseph Denby applied to the Parish for leave to have part of the gravel pit at Fairmile to build a cottage 'he being a pauper belonging to his parish'. Leave was granted and Denby Road, near Tartar Hill, now marks the site. More recently, gravel has been extracted for the construction of Esher and Cobham by-pass.

Cobham is in an area of low rainfall, the annual average being about 25 inches. The prevailing moisture-laden winds from the southwest deposit heavy rain, first on the South Downs, then on the Leith Hill range, and finally on the North Downs before reaching Cobham. It seems likely that the rainfall was much greater in Roman times, and areas such as the Tilt, which are now liable to flooding, were probably swamps or marshes.

Remains of nomadic prehistoric man have been found in different parts of Cobham. In 1965, a Mesolithic flint axe was discovered near the river and a polished flint axe was found near Norwood Farm in 1968. The first actual settlement in the area seems to have been on the higher terrace of the river in the vicinity of Leigh Hill.

Evidence of a settlement dating from the first century AD was found during the cutting of a carriage drive near the now demolished Appletons. Close by, in the grounds of Leigh Court, a Bronze Age burial was also discovered consisting of a cremation urn, about five inches high, in a small gravel pit. Any human ashes which the urn may have contained were emptied by the workmen who discovered it, in the vain hope of finding treasure. Also from the Bronze Age were the fragments of a hanging bowl found in the garden of Leigh Hill House, then the home of Mrs Bennett.

The later, Romano-British site consisted of a number of circular gravel pits whose original purpose was at first uncertain. It was thought that the pits had been used first as fireplaces and as refuse pits. However, as excavation proceeded in 1907, more pits were found which, when compared with similar sites in other parts of the country, seemed to represent a series of pit dwellings dating from the Bronze or Early Iron Age.

These contained fragments of hand-made and wheel-made pottery, the latter Roman. There were also loom weights from primitive weaving apparatus and pot-boilers, such as would have belonged to a British settlement of this type. The primitive houses of the people who lived here would have consisted of circular pits covered by low, thatched roofs. Further limited excavations of these sites took place in 1972 and 1973.

The community on the high ground above the river flood-plain seems to have continued for many centuries, and was probably the estate of Getinges recorded as part of the foundation grant given to Chertsey Abbey in 673 by Frithwald, Viceroy of Surrey. The name *Getinges* seems to have become 'Etynge in parochia de Coveham' in 1294 and by 1598 it was Yeatinge Fearme, now Eaton Grange on the Eaton Park estate.

The settlement of 673 may have been a stockaded enclosure. Beneath the hill lies the Tilt, which takes its name from the word *tilth* and which was then presumably the settlement's arable ground in Saxon times. A Saxon spear was found at Leigh Hill in 1926, close to the spot where the Bronze Age and Romano-British pottery had been discovered.

By the time of the Domesday survey, the name Getinges had given way to Coveham, implying that the prime settlement had then moved to the lower ground, where the parish church stands.

In 1932, during the construction of sewage works near Cobham Bridge, Roman pottery and wattle and daub fragments were found, which indicated occupation, with timber huts, about AD 50-100.

Substantial Roman remains were discovered at the southern end of the parish, near Chatley Farm, in 1942. These comprised a bath house of the later Roman period of c AD 350. Such bath houses were sometimes free-standing, but would normally be expected to have some association with a nearby villa or industrial process, such as the tile manufactory at nearby Ashtead. However, no such building was discovered, and it may well be that the river had destroyed any main villa that may have existed together with about a third of the bath building.

The building, once excavated, proved to be a normal bath house of which four rooms had survived: a coldbath, a warm room, a hot room and a sweating chamber. It was of amateur construction and ceased to be used soon after AD 360.

Other nearby Roman sites, outside the parish, are at Stoke D'Abernon and Ashtead.

The Domesday survey of 1085 was partly a feudal reckoning, partly a census, but chiefly an assessment of land value for taxation.

The survey of Cobham is as follows:

In ELMBRIDGE hundred

The Abbey hold COBHAM itself. Before 1066 it answered for 30 hides, now for 12½ hides. Land for 10 ploughs. In lordship (Cobham Court Farm) 1 plough;

29 villagers and 6 cottagers with 9 ploughs

3 mills worth 13s 4d; meadow 1 acre; woodland worth 40 pigs (that is for the right to run say 400 in the woods)

Value before 1066 £20, now £14.

William of Watteville holds 2 hides from the Abbey itself. An Englishman held them before 1066, and in King Edward's lifetime he gave this land to the church in alms. The land is in the manor of Esher. (Perhaps Norwood Farm)

6 villagers with 2 ploughs

Value before 1066 and now 14s 6d.

The population figures recorded in Domesday Book are probably households and it has been suggested that a multiplier of 4 or 5 should be used to obtain some indication of the total population at this time.

LEFT: The Bronze Age burial urn found at Leigh Hill, and BELOW: Leigh Hill from a postcard, c1905.

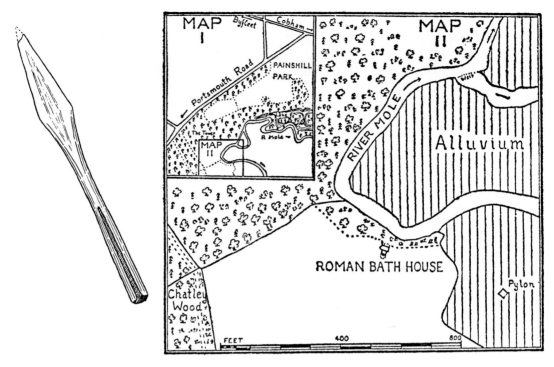

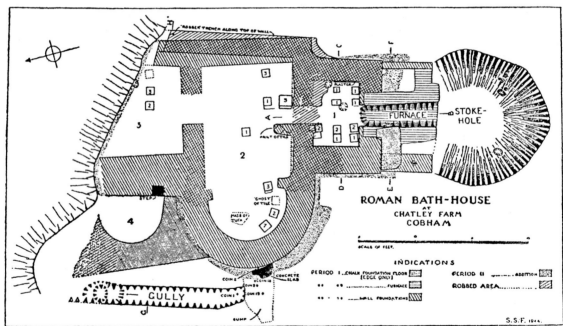

LEFT: Sketch of a Saxon spear found at Leigh Hill in 1926; RIGHT: site of
the late Roman Bath-House at Chatley Farm and BELOW: plan.

ABOVE: Pattern-stamped flue tiles from the Roman Bath-House at Chatley and BELOW: Roman pottery from the site of the former Cobham sewage works.

INSET: The conventual seal of Chertsey Abbey; ABOVE: extract from King Athelstan's Charter. During the Danish wars in AD 871 the Abbot and monks of Chertsey were killed, the Abbey burnt and the lands laid waste. The Abbey was refounded in AD 933 and a grant of lands, including Cobham, was confirmed by King Athelstan in that year.

ABOVE: Church Cobham (the High Street from the junction with Church
Street); CENTRE: Street Cobham (the Portsmouth Road outside the White
Lion); and BELOW: Tilt Cobham, all c1905. (The word Tilt comes from the
Saxon word *tilthe* and has nothing to do with knights in armour jousting on
the green, as local legend has it.)

ABOVE: Tartar Hill, c1905. Here were some of Cobham's gravel pits, used for surfacing the roads. BELOW: Old Downside Bridge showing damage caused by the 1968 floods.

ABOVE: A helicopter lands in Cobham Recreation Ground during the 1968 floods when Cobham was virtually cut off from the surrounding towns and villages, and BELOW: Mill Road by Cedar House.

John Carey's map of the Cobham district in 1786.

# Crossroads

The river Mole, which winds its way around Cobham, not only affected the development of the community but also its communications. The crossing of the river at Street Cobham was always important because of its position on the ancient road from Kingston to Guildford, shown on the Gough Map of c1360 as part of the main route from London to the West of England. At first, there must have been a ford, the road probably rising from the left bank of the river to run through the hollow at the foot of the hill to the south of Painshill House.

The Portsmouth Road has undoubtedly seen many great and famous people who have travelled this way. King John and his knights travelled through from Kingston in the year 1200 to spend Christmas in Guildford Castle. An inscription on the present Cobham bridge is based on a lost document of 1239, which is said to have stated that the first bridge on the site was built in 1100 by Matilda (Maud) of Scotland, Queen of Henry I, for the benefit of the soul of one of her maidens drowned in crossing the ford. The Queen gave land on the Cobham side of the river to maintain half the bridge while, on the Walton side, the lord of the manor did likewise. In 1239 Abraam was the bridge keeper and, in 1345, John le Smyth appears to have had a smithy by the bridge to shoe travellers' horses.

Responsibility for bridge maintenance continued to be shared between the manors of Cobham and Walton for many centuries, though not always in a satisfactory manner. In 1671 a naval commissioner wrote to his superiors that he had arrived late at his destination because Cobham Bridge was 'part carried away with the flood and the river too deep to pass through'.

In the eighteenth century, carriages were made to cross the ford unless the river had risen to a certain height. The bridge was locked and the key kept by the landlord of the former King's Arms. In 1779 Thomas Page, lord of the manor, was indicted for not repairing the Cobham half of the bridge. Eventually, in the 1780s the wooden bridge was replaced by one of brick which, though widened and repaired, still stands.

The architect of the new Cobham bridge was the County Surveyor, George Gwilt, who also rebuilt the bridge on the Downside road about this time. Downside bridge is heard of in 1415 when Thomas Freke bequeathed 2s for repairing 'Downbrygge' and in 1528, John Bygnold left 20d 'to making down bridge'. In the same century Robert Gavell of Cobham was involved in litigation over the maintenance of the bridge. There was a horse bridge here about 1760 when a new bridge for carriages was built. By 1769 it was in a dangerous state and a new one, designed by Gwilt, was completed by 1787. This survived intact until 1968, when it was badly damaged by severe flooding. The present bridge was opened in 1971.

Until the mid-eighteenth century, the roads in England were generally in a poor state and often impassable during the winter months. Most roads were maintained by the Parish and an unpaid surveyor was appointed, whose job it was to exact a fixed number of days' labour from the men of the parish. The Surrey Quarter Sessions of 1661 recorded that 'The highway at Fayre Myle end in Cobham, leading thence to Eshere, has been out of repair . . . ever since 1 Sept. 1661, so that the liege people of the king . . . cannot pass . . . without great danger, to their grave nuisance . . . The inhabitants of Cobham ought to repair it whenever necessary'. In 1688 Samuel Pepys recorded 'to Gilford, losing our way for three or four miles about Cobham'.

The first Turnpike Act was passed in the late 17th century, making a Turnpike Trust responsible for the maintenance of certain roads, and allowing it to exact tolls from users at certain points on the road. The Portsmouth Road was turnpiked in stages. Cobham was on the stretch between Kingston and Petersfield, which was turnpiked by Act of Parliament in 1749, and the Cobham Toll House stood between the White Lion and Cobham bridge, near the present Matthew Arnold Close. The Trust responsible for the section of highway passing through Cobham was wound up in 1873, and the toll house demolished.

The other great innovation of the eighteenth century, that did so much to stimulate travel and commerce, was the canals. During the latter part of the century there were several abortive schemes to cut a canal across Cobham from the Tilt to Norwood Farm. In 1792, Major William Abington of Cobham headed local objections to such a scheme, which would have formed part of a navigable canal from the Sussex coast to Dorking and then, by means of the river Mole, to the Thames.

Much of the road traffic during the eighteenth and early nineteenth centuries comprised commercial stage coaches. Cobham's Fairmile was a favourite spot for drivers since they could, for the first time out of London, get up some speed on this straight and firm (ie gravelly) stretch of road. The increase in passenger traffic brought an increase in highway robbery, especially in the lonely commons around Cobham. In 1577, five men attacked Jasper Swyfte and his servant 'in the highway at Cobham' and stole his horse, together with articles of gold and money. Mrs Balchin, who lived in Cedar House in the eighteenth century, was once robbed by a highwayman when travelling in her coach over the Fairmile Common.

The first mail coach was introduced in 1784 and the first post office in Cobham was near the White Lion. Local mail was delivered by paid letter-carriers. In 1861 Cobham had the distinction of the country's only qualified female letter carrier — Eliza Harris of Street Cobham.

With the advent of the railway, the mail was brought to Weybridge and then carted to Cobham. When Cobham station was opened later in the century, the post office moved to its present position in the High Street. The original building, erected by Post Master George Samuel White, now forms part of the sorting office. White was a strict disciplinarian, as is borne out by entries in his Day Book.

Another means of communication was provided by the tall brick tower on Chatley Heath — one of the best preserved of the old semaphore stations linking Portsmouth to the Admiralty in London. The master station at Portsmouth kept in touch with ships in the harbour by a signalling system not unlike that used on the railways. A chain of such semaphore stations was constructed in the 1820s at intervals of between five and ten miles on vantage points such as Pewley Down at Guildford, Telegraph Hill at Hinchley Wood and Putney Heath. The system was replaced in 1847 by the electric telegraph.

The tower, which is central to the theme of Warwick Deeping's novel *The Woman at the Door* (1937) became a private home, the Johnson family the last occupants. This unique tower is now owned by Surrey County Council. Hopefully it will be restored and access granted so the public may enjoy the extensive views over Richmond Park, the North Downs and Windsor Castle.

The terrace of early nineteenth century cottages in Between Streets, called Post Boys Row, was probably associated, not with mail deliveries but with the form of transport known as posting. Local innkeepers would hire out either post chaises and post boys on a mileage basis, or just the horses. The post boys were usually dressed to a standard pattern which, in the south of England, comprised a bright yellow jacket, breeches, short top boots and a large beaver hat. Most postboys were a good deal older than their name suggests, and they invariably received their keep from the innkeeper, and their income from tips. In the 1820s the White Lion was said to be one of the best posting inns in the Kingdom.

In 1836, the year when the coaching trade was at its peak, some twenty different coaches, including the Royal Mail, passed through Cobham from London to Guildford, Southampton, Chichester and Portsmouth. They carried such romantic and evocative names as *The Star of Brunswick, The Royal Sussex, The Red Rover, The Rocket* and *The Royal Blue.*

But the demise of coaching was in sight with the advent of 'the permanent way'. The first railway passenger service in the world had been opened between Liverpool and Manchester in 1830. The author of *Rambles by Rivers* (1844) wrote 'Cobham-street; — a place that prior to the opening of the South-Western Railway had a lively bustling appearance, very different from that it now wears'.

In 1861, the barrister-poet A.J. Munby stayed at the White Lion and spent a pleasant evening in the bar chatting to local tradesmen. He recorded in his journal of how they talked 'of the coaching days, when the White Lion, then twice as big, kept forty horses, and 27 coaches passed to Portsmouth every day, and the shoemaker, who was then ostler, saved thirty pounds in his first year'.

On a later visit to Cobham, Munby observed a new use to which the Portsmouth Road had been put — 'cycling: 'Many bicyclists en route: about 12 young women among them, of who 3 wore breeches and rode astride'. The Ripley Road, as it was known to the 'cyclists, became a popular haunt and local tradesmen benefitted from the visitors. Cobham had at least one 'cycling club of its own and there were various repair shops and refreshment rooms *en route.* The landlord of the White Lion, during the closing years of the last century, was 'Bath Road' Smith, a famous 'cyclist and member of the Bath Road Cycling Club which often used the Ripley Road for excursions. The Fairmile was the venue for 'cycle racing as early as 1870.

Carriers also plied their trade between nearby villages as did the local omnibus. An 1879 enquiry into a proposed railway scheme for Cobham referred to an omnibus which ran from Ripley to Esher Station to meet the 9 am train to London. The fare from Cobham to Esher was one shilling — a large sum in those days, and inevitably a great number of people made the journey on foot. William Worsfold, a local farmer, who lived at Ham Manor (then Spencer House), when asked if he considered the proposed scheme to be a good thing, replied 'If you had to ride from Cobham to Esher on our omnibus you would think it a very great advantage'.

There were several abortive attempts to bring the railway into Cobham in the middle of the last century. Two schemes included proposals for a station in Cobham on the site of Oakdene Parade, near the Post Office. Only one of these schemes got as far as a House of Lords enquiry before being dropped, and this was the 1869 proposal to construct a narrow gauge line between Esher and Cobham. The chief promoters were Charles Combe and William Worsfold. Combe was anxious to provide his estate at Cobham Park with coal, which was at that time brought by barge to Thames Ditton and then carted to Cobham. The line would also assist in transporting farm produce to the markets at Kingston and London. Worsfold, a Churchwarden and Surveyor of the Parish, confirmed that the local people were much in favour of the scheme.

The chief objector was John Earley Cook of Oxshott who was concerned that his coach and four (one of the few in the district), would not be able to negotiate the proposed level crossing at Fairmile Lane. He was also concerned about the inevitable (and detrimental) increase in population.

The enquiry gave no reason why the scheme was abandoned but the *Surrey Advertiser* referred to the Court Circular, which stated that Sir Thomas Biddulph intended to oppose the scheme on behalf of Queen Victoria, who considered that the proposed line would pass too close to her estate at nearby Claremont, and would be an intrusion into her privacy.

The present railway station on the Waterloo-Guildford line was opened on 2 February 1885. In its first year the journey to London took 51 minutes. The first local railway accident appears to have taken place ten years later when Joseph Robbins of Paddington was knocked down on the line and his 'fearfully mutilated body' found near the station. The Cobham line was electrified in 1925.

The Portsmouth Road regained its former importance with the invention of the internal combustion engine. One of the first motor cars seen in Cobham was reported in the *Parish Magazine* in 1897 as 'what at first seemed . . . a very ugly bicycle, but which we soon made out to be a small vehicle on four wheels, containing two people seated one in front of the other. A strong and disagreeable smell of petroleum oil at once revealed that we were watching one of the most recent inventions of this go-ahead age. The car was flying along at the rate of about twelve miles an hour, and we were much struck with the remarkably easy manner in which it was turned round for a retracing of the way, when the occupants discovered at the Tilt, that they had taken the wrong direction. The roads were dirty at the time and both car and riders were splashed all over with mud. We agree with the many who think that it will be a distant future before these motor carriages become at all popular'.

An earlier *Parish Magazine* had referred to a problem which seems more synonymous with the present century. The subject was damage to buildings caused by 'the practice of driving heavy agricultural engines through the streets at high speed'. The report continued 'It is no secret that the ancient and picturesque buildings of Church Cobham are beginning to suffer from the finger of time, and the neglect of beings dignified by the name of landlords. If to these is added the destructive forces of the demon engine, Church Cobham will be laid in ruins long before its time. . . . when these heavy traction engines rush past the whole building trembles from garrett to cellar — and recently the new pipes laid by the water company were found to be fractured. If these peripatetic earthquakes are allowed to continue their Mazeppa-like career unmolested, very serious injury to buildings will inevitably ensue'.

The Cobham Garage (formerly the Kings Arms and now replaced by the Murco Service Station) was one of the Automobile Association's earliest agents. The roads around Cobham are linked firmly with the history of the AA.

Although the first AA 'cyclist patrols covered the London-Brighton Road in 1905, it was not long before these were extended to the Portsmouth Road. The Surrey police were particularly active in setting up speed traps on the road between Kingston and Petersfield, and that stretch from Esher to Cobham including the Fairmile was the most notorious.

In AA annals this section of the road is most famous, because of the prosecution of a patrol accused of obstructing the police, when warning motorists of the existence of a speed trap in September 1905. He was later arrested on a charge of perjury. Fortunately he was acquitted, but the 'Fairmile Case' as it became known, was one of the first of many occasions when the AA and its patrols appeared in the dock.

A similar prosecution resulted in the adoption of the famous AA salute to members, to indicate that the road was free of police traps: this was in 1909.

Between the two world wars, plans were made for the construction of a great orbital road around the south of London, that would have run close to the route of the M25 motorway currently under construction. There was talk in the 1960s of widening the High Street and, as a result, the delightful cottages on the narrow bend of River Hill were demolished and a dual carriage way made. Fortunately, the plan got no further but already Cobham had lost a number of its older buildings. The next plan was to pedestrianise the High Street and create an inner ring road. The road across Leg Of Mutton Field and that linking Between Streets and Anyards Road was part of this scheme, but the final stage of opening up Cedar Road and taking traffic out onto Mill Road, near Cedar House, was never implemented and, no doubt, never will be now that Cobham's riverside area is a conservation area.

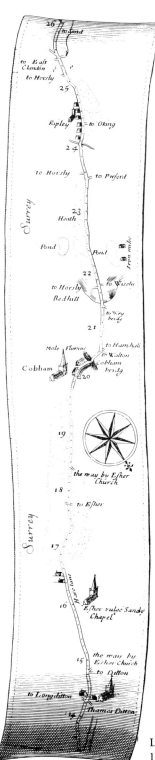

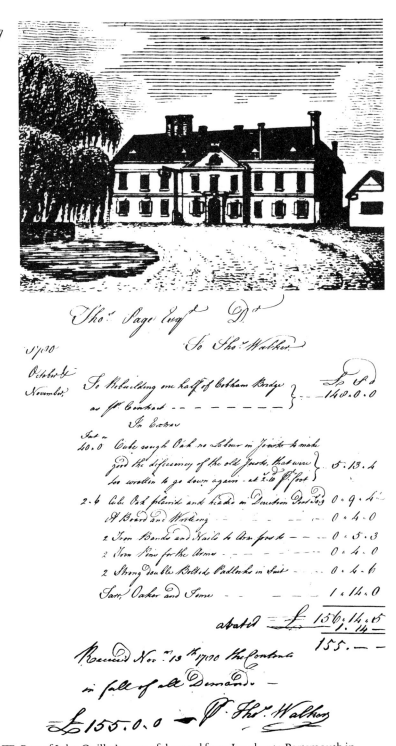

LEFT: Part of John Ogilby's map of the road from London to Portsmouth in 1675. The first town plan of Cobham. ABOVE: The White Lion in 1830. Described as one of the best posting inns in the Kingdom. BELOW: Bill for work done at Cobham Bridge in 1780.

ABOVE: Cobham Bridge by J. Hassell in 1823. The building on the right is
the King's Arms, seen BELOW: c1905. The key to the old Cobham Bridge
was kept here.

ABOVE: *The Red Rover;* one of the many coaches that passed through
Cobham in the 1820s, and BELOW: 'An Extraordinary Scene On The
Portsmouth Road' by T. Rowlandson.

LEFT: Old Downside Bridge before the 1968 floods; RIGHT: the Semaphore Tower on Chatley Heath from a photograph taken in the 1950s, and BELOW: Leigh Place Hotel, c1910. This house, which stood opposite the river, was the home of Major William Abington, who headed the list of objectors to a proposal to cut a canal across Cobham in the late eighteenth century.

ABOVE: Cobham Post Office c1905, Post Master George Samuel White, centre. BELOW: Mr Weller's Fly c1900 — Cobham's original taxi service.

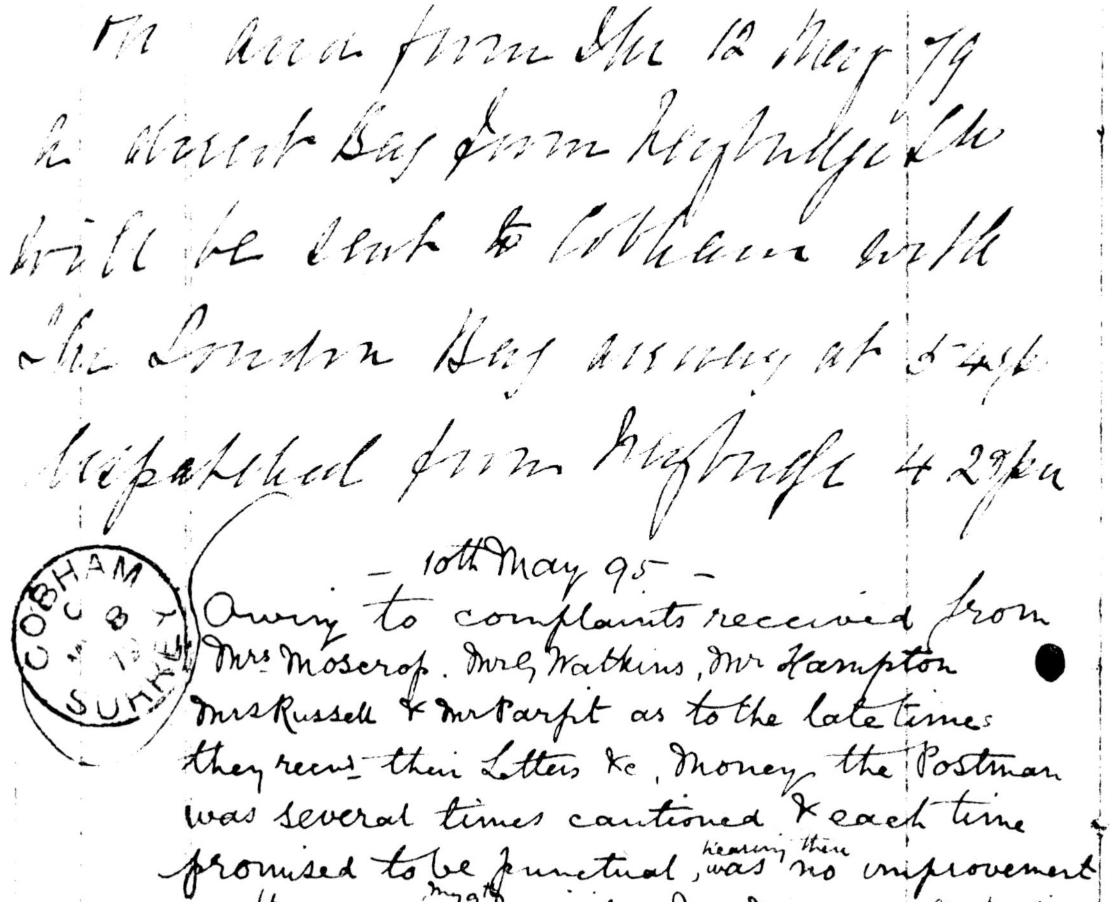

[illegible] from the 12 May 79
[illegible] Bag from Weybridge [illegible]
will be sent to Cobham with
the London Bag arriving at 5.45p
dispatched from Weybridge 4.29pm

COBHAM C 8 [illegible] SURREY

— 10th May 95 —
Owing to complaints received from Mrs Moscrop. Mrs Watkins, Mr Hampton Mrs Russell & Mr Parfit as to the late times they recvd their Letters &c, Money the Postman was several times cautioned & each time promised to be punctual, hearing there was no improvement in the service May 9th I visited Mrs Moscrop, Mr Parfitt & went to [illegible] House [illegible] Servant to ascertain if such the case & found out he was very late in delivery, On the 10th May 8 55 am I found him in the Stable Yard of the Hut Hotel conversing with two men 8 Letters for Fellside Cottages in his pouch which Should have been delivd before the Hut Hotel & as the 8 Letters would not be delivd before 9-20 instead of 8-20 am I dismissed him at 6.55 PM & put J. Gibbins Telegraph Messenger on the duty 11th May to Start from Head Office 6 40 am arrive Lower Lodge 7-20 = as authorised time

An extract from the Post Master's Day Book showing the strong disciplinary action that could be taken against postmen. This particular postman was found 'in the stable yard of the Hut Hotel (Wisley) conversing with two men' when he still had letters to deliver.

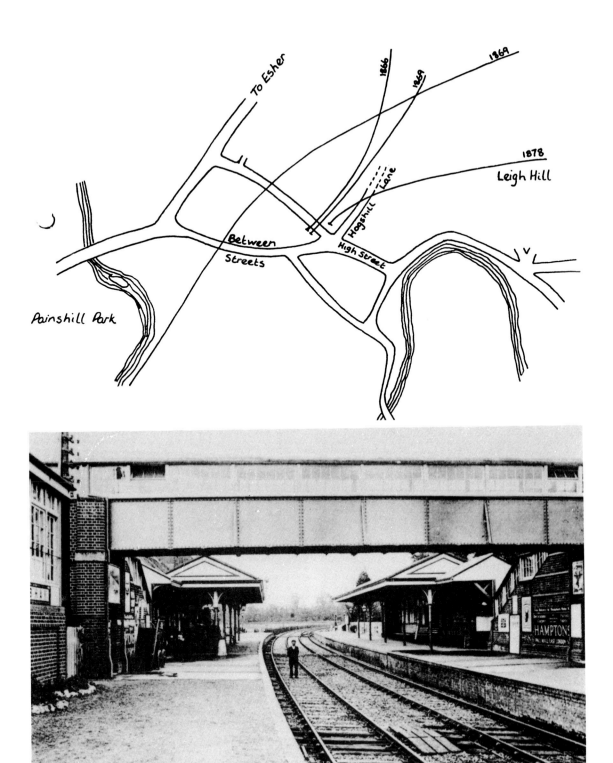

ABOVE: Various projected railway schemes, and BELOW: Cobham Railway Station at the beginning of the century.

# L. & S. W. R. TIME TABLE.

| UP—WEEK DAYS. | a. m. | a. m. | a. m. | p. m. | p. m. | p. m. | p. m. | SUNDAYS. a. m. | p. m. |
|---|---|---|---|---|---|---|---|---|---|
| Guildford .......... | 7.25 | 8.40 | 10.28 | 12.35 | 4.40 | 7.0 | 8.52 | 8.55 | 7.30 |
| „ London Rd. | 7.29 | 8.44 | 10.32 | 12.39 | 4.44 | 7.4 | 8.56 | 8.59 | 7.34 |
| Clandon ........... | 7.36 | 8.51 | 10.38 | 12.45 | 4.51 | 7.11 | 9.3 | 9.5 | 7.40 |
| Horsley ........... | 7.43 | 8.58 | 10.46 | 12.52 | 4.58 | 7.18 | 9.10 | 9.12 | 7.47 |
| Effingham Junction | 7.47 | 9.2 | 10.50 | 12.56 | 5.2 | 7.22 | 2.14 | 9.15 | 7.51 |
| Cobham .......... | 7.52 | 9.7 | 10.55 | 1.1 | 5.7 | 7.27 | 9.19 | 9.20 | 7.56 |
| Oxshott .......... | 7.57 | 9.12 | 10.59 | 1.5 | 5.14 | 7.31 | 9.24 | 9.24 | 8.0 |
| Claygate .......... | 8.2 | 9.17 | 11.4 | 1.10 | 5.21 | 7.36 | 9.29 | 9.29 | 8.5 |
| Surbiton .......... | 8.9 | 9.24 | 11.10 | 1.17 | 5.30 | 7.42 | 9.36 | 9.41 | 8.27 |
| Wimbledon ....... | .. | .. | .. | .. | .. | .. | 9.46 | 9.54 | 8.39 |
| Clapham Junction .. | .. | .. | .. | 1.33 | 5.46 | 7.58 | 9.53 | 10.2 | 8.47 |
| Waterloo........... | 8.37 | 9.52 | 11.33 | 1.45 | 5.58 | 8.10 | 10.5 | 10.14 | 8.59 |

| DOWN—WEEK DAYS. | a. m. | a. m. | p. m. | p. m. | p. m. | p. m. | p. m. | p. m. | SUNDAYS. a. m. | p. m. |
|---|---|---|---|---|---|---|---|---|---|---|
| Waterloo........... | 6.20 | 9.25 | 12.35 | 2.32 | 3.40 | 5.25 | 6.20 | 8.45 | 9.50 | 8.30 |
| Clapham Junction .. | 6.31 | 9.35 | 12.45 | 2.42 | .. | .. | 6.29 | 8.56 | 10.2 | .. |
| Wimbledon ....... | 6.39 | 9.43 | 12.52 | 2.49 | .. | .. | .. | 9.6 | 10.10 | .. |
| Surbiton .......... | 6.49 | 9.53 | 1.2 | 2.59 | .. | 5.49 | 6.47 | 9.18 | 10.30 | 9.0 |
| Claygate .......... | 6.56 | 10.0 | 1.8 | 3.5 | .. | 5.55 | 6.53 | 9.24 | 10.39 | 9.6 |
| Oxshott .......... | 7.2 | 10.5 | 1.13 | 3.10 | .. | 6.0 | 6.58 | 9.29 | 10.46 | 9.11 |
| Cobham .......... | 7.7 | 10.10 | 1.18 | 3.15 | 4.8 | 6.5 | 7.3 | 9.34 | 10.53 | 9.15 |
| Effingham Junction.. | 7.12 | 10.15 | 1.23 | 3.20 | .. | 6.10 | 7.8 | 9.39 | 10.59 | 9.19 |
| Horsley .......... | 7.16 | 10.19 | 1.27 | 3.24 | .. | 6.14 | 7.12 | 9.43 | 11.4 | 9.23 |
| Clandon .......... | 7.23 | 10.26 | 1.36 | 3.30 | .. | 6.20 | 7.18 | 9.49 | 11.12 | 9.29 |
| Guildford London Rd. | 7.29 | 10.33 | 1.42 | 3.36 | .. | 6.26 | 7.24 | 9.55 | 11.18 | 9.36 |
| Guildford .......... | 7.33 | 10.37 | 1.46 | 3.40 | 4.23 | 6.30 | 7.28 | 9.59 | 11.22 | 9.40 |

ABOVE: Local railway timetable for 1890. CENTRE: Early motor traffic on the Portsmouth Road, outside the White Lion in the days of C.A. 'Bath Road' Smith, c1905, and BELOW: from opposite the Cottage Hospital, c1910.

ABOVE: Cobham Garage (formerly The King's Arms and now replaced by the Murco Petrol Filling Station). The garage was one of the AA's earliest agents and in this night shot taken in 1909 the AA Road Manager, George Lambert, is beside the driver of the Gladiator car. BELOW: The Old Oak Tree Restaurant on the corner of Copse Road and Portsmouth Road, c1910.

Cobham Cycling Club taken around the turn of the century. One of these gentlemen is C.A. 'Bath Road' Smith.

# Manor & Parish

In the early Middle Ages, local administration and land ownership were largely in the hands of the manorial lords. Petty offences were punished by the manorial courts and there were manorial constables to keep the peace.

In Cobham, the lord had the right to take fines for releasing stray animals from the Pound, a wooden fenced enclosure, which in early times stood by what is now Cobham Park, opposite the end of Plough Lane. In more recent times, the Pound was on the green by the entrance to Cobham Court near Downside Bridge. The pinder, or pound keeper was elected by the manorial court. Other rights of the lord were the right to 'waif', or abandoned property, and 'pannage' which was revenue from his tenants' pigs on the common.

The tenants' land holdings were in the Common Fields — large enclosures divided into narrow strips called furlongs.

The village geese were driven to Goose Green, off the Horsley Road near Downside, along Downside Road, formerly known as Poultry Lane.

In a survey of the Manor of Cobham made by Ralph Agas in 1598, the names of the common fields were stated to be North Field, Church Field, Appleton Field, West Croft, Down Field, Puntington Field and Rewoorthe. Church Field lay between the church, Street Cobham and Hogshill, and was thus responsible for keeping separate the communities of Street Cobham and Church Cobham until recent times.

In addition to land in the Common Fields, tenants also had rights to graze cattle on the waste or common land such as the Old Common and the Tilt. The manorial court elected constables and tithing men for Street Cobham, Church Cobham and Downside.

A manor might cover the same area as the Parish, but in other cases the Parish might contain more than one manor. In Cobham there were the manors of Cobham and Down as well as parts of the manor of Ham in Chertsey. No manorial records seem to have survived for the manor of Down and it seems to have merged with the manor of Cobham in the early eighteenth century. For many years both the manors of Cobham and Down were in the ownership of Chertsey Abbey, and Frithwald's grant was gradually enlarged by gift or exchange. However, in 1537, when Henry VIII dissolved the monasteries, the manor of Cobham was handed over to the Crown for £5,000.

Cobham Court, the manor house, still stands, though much altered over the centuries. In 1331 Abbot John de Rutherwyck of Chertsey repaired the Chamber at Cobham and added a new chapel. Until the dissolution of the Abbey, a bailiff would have managed the manor from Cobham Court, assisted by a rent collector. James Sutton 'bayle of this lordshyppe' died in 1530 and his son, Richard, appears to have been the last steward. After James' death, his wife Elizabeth appears to have married George Bigley, and it was this couple who acquired the manor from Queen Mary in 1553, together with Cobham Court Farm, Church House and Cobham Mill, for £1,092 14s.

The manor of Cobham passed from George Bigley to his daughter Dorothy, who married Robert Gavell. Robert's great grandson Vincent married Margaret Lynde, daughter of the famous divine, Sir Humphrey Lynde. After Robert's death, Margaret married John Platt, the arch-opponent of Gerrard Winstanley and the Diggers.

Vincent Gavell's son, Robert, acquired the manor of Cobham and in 1708 it passed from the Gavell family to Lady Frances Lanesborough, who purchased Downe Place, thereby merging the two manors. Cobham Court remained in the Gavell family and descended to the Wood family in the middle of the last century. It is now the home of Charles Combe.

The manor of Cobham passed from Lady Lanesborough's heirs to Thomas Page of Pointers in 1779. Pointers now became the manor house and William Bray, the historian of Surrey, had become Steward of the Manor in 1770 and recorded in his diary that on 14 September 1781 he breakfasted at Pointers. Thomas Page's son of the same name purchased the manor and set about enlarging the house and improving the grounds. He entertained members of the Royal family at Pointers, including Frederick, Duke of York.

The Page family continued to live at Pointers until the middle of the last century when their descendants, the Mounts, inherited the manor holding, until manorial jurisdiction came to an end under a general Act of Parliament.

By early Tudor times local administration fell on the parishes. The manorial constables were replaced by parish officers and the parish was required to appoint a surveyor of the highways and an overseer of the poor who were elected at public meeting of the parishioners, commonly called a vestry.

The Cobham Vestry Book, which dates from 1770, shows that despite its name the Vestry met for many years, not in the church, but in local public houses such as the White Lion, the Running Mare, the White Hart, the Bear, the Crown and the George. It was not until 1797 that a meeting was held 'to take into consideration the propriety of Building a Vestry Room in order to curtail the expense of holdings Vestrys at a Public House'.

Poor relief was the chief matter dealt with by the Vestry. A poor rate was agreed twice a year and two Overseers were appointed. So long as the poor remained few in number, the Parish preferred to pass them relief in money and goods, but when they became more numerous, it was found more economical to maintain them on a communal basis in a workhouse. Cobham's Workhouse was on the Tilt and seems to have originally comprised a property called Tilt Hatch, as well as a number of other cottages. A master was installed by the Parish on an annual contract and in 1801, when the poor rate was fixed at 3s 6d in the pound, it was agreed that 'Mr. Griffith is to make, wash and mend for the Poor'. The following year, the Workhouse was let to Griffith for one year 'at the sum of £620 to Feed and Cloathe all the poor that may at any time be sent into the Workhouse, all the outpays and every casualty that may happen relative to the poor, Broken Bones, Small Pox and Insane Persons excepted, Mr. Griffith to receive all the benefit of the Paupers Work'. In 1809, the poor rate rose to five shillings.

In addition to providing accommodation in the Workhouse, the Parish would often 'farm out' the poor to anyone who had enough accommodation and who would maintain them for a fixed *per capita* payment. In 1786 it was agreed 'That if Port will take King's child from the Workhouse he shall be allowed one shilling pr. week'. Often young men would be apprenticed out from the Workhouse and in 1775 it was agreed 'That Mr. Raby (of Downside Mill) do take Benjamin son of Richard Bullen Deceased, To put him Apprentice for seven years to one of his men'.

The stigma of being a parish pauper was emphasised in 1797 when it was ordered 'that a Badge containing the Mark C.P. (ie Cobham Parish) in scarlet cloth be affixed on the clothes of every pauper in the workhouse and that the children . . . be taught to read'. In 1825 it was resolved that the Workhouse inmates should not in future be allowed to go in and out of the place as they pleased without the Master's consent 'and that the parish officer take means to inclose the premises'.

36

The maintenance of the poor was a heavy burden on parishioners, and vagrants and paupers from other parishes were sent back to their place of 'settlement'. In 1771 it was decided that 'all persons that inhabit and work in our Parish not being Parishioners, without security shall be immediately ordered to bring certificates or be removed'.

Illigitimate children were also a burden on the poor rate and, in 1786, it was agreed that 'the Officers do as soon as convenient execute the Warrant that they have got upon Dr. Trusler for a Bastard sworn to him by his Maid'.

Payment both in kind and money was made to the deserving poor and an example of the former is to be found in 1775 when 'Richard Collingham's Girl at Mr. Woods' was given 'a pr. of shoes 2 shifts a pr. stockings an apron and under petticoat and Gown 2 aprons & Hankerchive a pr. of stays & a pr. of pattens'.

In 1799, during a period of high prices, the Vestry resolved that the Master 'should use a proportion of one third Rye Flour with the Flour used in making bread at the Workhouse'.

The Vestry could engage a doctor to attend certain poor people and in 1781 it was agreed that 'Doctor Lamb be allowed to attend Batt's Daughter one month longer from this time in order to make a cure if he can'. In 1820 there was a smallpox scare and it was resolved that to prevent the increase of the disease 'such of the poor belonging to this parish as may be induced to be inoculated for the cowpock may be applying to Mr. Brown be vacinated — who has agreed to perform the operation at 5 shilling each'.

A Pest House was maintained for people suffering from contagious diseases and, in 1783, it was let to William Atkins at the rent of £3 per annum and 'if there shall be any person with the smallpox carried to the said house He shall be allowed Ten shillings pr. week and all necessarys as usual at the said house'. The Pest House stood on Pointers Green in Ockham Lane, near the new crossing of the M25 motorway.

Defence of the realm was the Vestry's concern in 1803 and the Parish agreed to bear the 'expense of Arming and Clothing' those who volunteered their services in the event of a French invasion.

Maintenance of the highways was another responsibility and surveyors or 'waywardens' were appointed for Church Cobham, Street Cobham and Downside. Each man in the parish had to perform a fixed number of days' labour in repairing the roads. In 1799 it was agreed 'that whereas Mr. Davis has made application for a Road to be made to his house from Mr. Freeland's farm to Norwood Farm, and whereas Mr. Davis was now in arrears six days Duty, it was agreed that he shall be excused the 6 days duty in consequence of his making the said road'.

In 1831, Henry Worsfold, Permanent Overseer, objected to the allowance made to him for executing his office, and it was resolved that 'in addition he be in future allowed the labour of one of the boys from the Workhouse without being charged anything for such boy's employment'.

Under the 1834 Poor Law Act, Poor Law Unions under elected boards of guardians replaced the many parish units and, in 1836, the Cobham Vestry resolved that it would be 'most advantageous for this parish to be united under the new Poor Law Act with Epsom Union'.

Cobham's poor were eventually transferred to Epsom, and the Parish Workhouse on the Tilt together with 'eight brick built slated tenements' which had been built nearby in 1822, and 'six freehold brick and tiled tenements' near the Running Mare, were sold to Henry Worsfold. Number 9 and 10 Korea Cottages are believed to be the last of the Parish cottages.

One indirect result of the 1834 Act was the fostering of self-dependence which was manifested in increased membership in the local Friendly Societies. In 1838 the United Brothers Benefit Society met at the Kings Arms.

In 1833 the Vestry had resolved 'that a school-room for the poor in the principles of the Established Church be built on the Parish ground at the North end of the Tilt'. This building later became a parish room, then a fire engine house and is now used as a warehouse.

Parish policing by elected constables was unpaid, generally unpopular and sometimes dangerous. Many of the Constables' duties were scarcely 'police' matters and included those more appropriate to the Overseers. In 1824 the Parish of Cobham was fined by the Court Leet for not having any cage or stocks and it was agreed to 'build a cage at the south end of the almshouse on the Tilt'. However, this plan was not carried through and, in 1829, a further resolution was made 'that a new cage be made on an octagonal plan with a domed ceiling on the old common near the Royal Oak' from plans prepared by Mr Dallen. The office of Parish Constable disappeared in 1872. The Vestry remained the common form of local administration until well into the nineteenth century.

ABOVE: Cobham Court in 1822 from a watercolour by J. Hassell. The house still stands, not far from Downside Bridge. LEFT: The arms of the Gavell family who were, for many years, the lords of the Manor of Cobham and RIGHT: William Bray, the Surrey historian and Steward of the Manor of Cobham, from a portrait of 1832 by John Linnell.

*Bear at Cobham April 15th 1781*

|  | £ | s | d |
|---|---|---|---|
| Dinner | 2 | 13 | 4 |
| Wine | 1 | 7 | 6 |
| Beer | 1 | 6 |  |
| Dressing |  | 5 |  |
| Horses |  | 1 |  |

*Same time Received the above in full Sarah Doranton* £5.. 12.. 10
2.. 8
5. 15. 10

*John Simpkinson Vicar*

*Carhampton*

*Thomas Page*

*John Balchin*

*Wm Spencer*

ABOVE: Receipt for manorial court dinners held at the Bear in 1781; LEFT: Work House cottages and RIGHT: Cobham School (later the Fire Station) and Almshouse — both on Cobham Tilt c1870. BELOW: Extract from Cobham Vestry Book, April 1809 — signatures of leading parishioners such as John Simpkinson (Vicar), Lord Carhampton of Cobham Park, Thomas Page (Lord of the Manor), William Spencer of Ham Manor and John Balchin of Cedar House.

# PARISH OF COBHAM.

## Notice is hereby given,

That a VESTRY MEETING of the Inhabitants of this Parish will be held at the Parochial School Rooms, in the said Parish, on Thursday, the 24th day of May, 1888, at the hour of 7.30 in the Afternoon, for the following purposes, namely :—

1st.—To consider a proposal of Thomas Henry Bennett, of Cobham Court, to dedicate to the use of the Public a certain Highway situate in the said Parish, leading from the Portsmouth Road to the road running from Street Cobham to Church Cobham and known as Anyards Road, of the length of 440 yards or thereabouts as the same is described in the plan deposited at the residence of Mr. John Ledger, Street Cobham, in the said Parish, and thereon coloured Red.

2nd.—To authorize the Kingston Highway Board as the Surveyors of Highways of the Parish of Cobham, to sell the exhausted Gravel Pit, situate at Fairmile, in the Parish of Cobham, and containing 3 acres of land, or thereabouts.

3rd.—To authorize the said Kingston Highway Board to expend the monies to be derived from the sale of the said Gravel Pit, or so much thereof as may be necessary, in and about the making of a new and more commodious Road or approach to the Cobham Railway Station, and in purchasing the necessary land for making such approach, and all other expenses incident and relating thereto.

A plan of the proposed new approach is also deposited as above.

Dated the 15th day of May, 1888.

WILLIAM ATTLEE,        } Churchwardens of the
THOMAS SWEETLOVE,      } Parish of Cobham,

Cobham Vestry Notice, 1888.

ABOVE: An election group outside the Crown in Cobham High Street c1880. The posters on the back of the carriages read 'Plump For Pennington' while a torn poster on the wall says 'Vote For Cubit'; BELOW: Two postcards — 'Awaiting the election results in Cobham January 21st 1910' the great crowd outside the Unionist Committee Room on River Hill and the Radical Committee Room in Marshall's Dairy Shop (part of the former Gammons building in the High Street).

# Cobham Women's Constitutional Association
## 1934—1935

*President*—MRS. COMBE.
*Chairman*—LADY FIRTH.   *Vice-Chairman*—MRS. MERCER.
*Hon. Treasurer*—MRS. C. A. GORDON CLARK.   *Hon. Secretary*—MRS. RICKMAN.
*Hon. Registrar*—MRS. J. HASLOCH.

*Committee*—

MRS. ATKINSON, MISS BISHOP, MISS CHADWICK, MRS. C. H. COMBE, THE LADY EBBISHAM, MRS. GOODBODY, MRS. GOLDS, MRS. GREENHOW, MRS. KENNARD, MRS. R. C. LEE, MRS. LEUCHARS, MRS. LUCAS, MRS. MACE, LADY McALPINE, MRS. McLACHLAN, MISS MOUNT, MRS. OSMAN, MRS. PRICE, MRS. REDFERN, MRS. RICHARDS, MRS. STERICKER, MRS. TALBOT, MRS. TALBOT-WILLCOX, MRS. THOMPSON, MRS. THORPE.

## Afternoon Meetings

*TUESDAY, OCTOBER 2nd, at 2.45 p.m.* :

**The Village Hall. Speaker : Commander A. R. J. Southby, R.N., M.P. : " What the Government has done."**
**Entertainment by Hazel School of Dancing (Miss W. Sayers). Tea.**

---

*TUESDAY, NOVEMBER 6th, at 2.15 p.m.* :

The Parish Room. Speaker : Mrs. Tead— " Communist Teaching to Children." Tea.

---

*TUESDAY, DECEMBER 4th, at 2.45 p.m.* :

**The Village Hall. ENTERTAINMENT and SALE OF WORK. Admittance by ticket, 3d.**

---

*TUESDAY, JANUARY 1st, 1935, at 3 p.m.*

**The Village Hall. CHILDREN'S PARTY by invitation to children of members.**

---

*TUESDAY, FEBRUARY 5th, at 2.45 p.m.* :

Parish Room. Speaker from Headquarters : " Local Government." Tea.

---

*TUESDAY, MARCH 5th, at 2.30 p.m.* :

**The Village Hall. The Annual General Meeting. Speaker : Captain Rex Davis, M.C., and an Entertainment (Tea free).**

## Whist Drives & Bridge Parties

*TUESDAY, OCTOBER 16th, at 2.30 p.m.* :

WHIST DRIVE. Tickets (including tea) 1/-. The Parish Room.

*Nov : 16th*

*FRIDAY, OCTOBER 19th, at 2.30 p.m.* :

**BRIDGE PARTY, open to all, by kind permission of Lady Firth, to be held at Hatchford Park. Tables 10/- each.**

---

*TUESDAY, NOVEMBER 20th, at 2.30 p.m.* :

WHIST DRIVE. Tickets (including tea) 1/-. The Parish Room.

---

*FRIDAY, DECEMBER 14th, at 2.30 p.m.* :

**BRIDGE PARTY, open to all, by kind permission of Mrs. Combe, to be held at Pains Hill. Tables 10/- each.**

---

*FRIDAY, DECEMBER 21st, at 8 p.m.* :

**The Village Hall. XMAS WHIST DRIVE for men and women members only. Tickets (including refreshments) 1/6. All proceeds to go to Divisional funds. First eight eligible to compete in Grand Divisional Whist Drive in March.**

---

*The following will be held in the Parish Room* :
*TUESDAY, JANUARY 15th, 1935, at 2.30 p.m.* :
WHIST DRIVE. Tickets (including tea) 1/-.

---

*TUESDAY, FEBRUARY 19th, at 2.30 p.m.* :
WHIST DRIVE. Tickets (including tea) 1/-.

---

*TUESDAY, MARCH 19th, at 2.30 p.m.* :
WHIST DRIVE. Tickets (including tea) 1/-.

Cobham Women's Constitutional Association 1934-1935.

# A Sacred Place

As in many of our towns and villages, the oldest surviving building in Cobham is the parish church. St Andrew's is a building of mixed style and periods which, together with the surrounding churchyard, presents a unique memorial to the many hundreds of people who, down the centuries, have made their homes in Cobham and who have been baptised, married and buried here.

From the earliest times Chertsey Abbey, who held the manor of Cobham, had the right to appoint an incumbent to the living. Although it was more usual for monastic houses, and later lay people, to appropriate the great tithe and appoint a deputy or vicar to fulfil the tasks of a rector, this did not happen at Cobham until 1465, when the monks obtained a licence from the Bishop of Winchester to take such action and endow a perpetual vicarage at Cobham.

The earliest known rector of Cobham was Aymer de Fureth who was appointed about 1166. The early rectors, and later the vicars, seem to have been men of some substance and learning.

The present building was founded in about 1150 and, although not recorded in Domesday Book, it is possible that an earlier church stood on the site. The original structure consisted of chancel, nave and tower. About fifty years later the chancel was extended eastwards and the Chantry built on the north side.

Of the original building, the most outstanding survival is the Norman doorway to the south aisle which is one of the finest in Surrey. Its elaborate design is of three rows of zig-zag and billet mouldings with a detached pillar on each side of its outer face. This doorway was moved to its present position in 1854, when the south aisle was added to the church. It is an inspiring thought that this doorway has been used as the main entrance to the church for over 800 years, and through it have passed many interesting and colourful personalities. The massive oak door is also worth notice with its fine iron hinges, made by Richard Lee in his forge at Street Cobham some 130 years ago.

The plainness of the massive Norman tower may indicate that it is a little older than the more elaborate south doorway. It is square in plan and contains two floors. The tower walls are three and a half feet thick and built of rubble, pudding stone and flint. Incredible though it may seem, the tower is built on sand, without any foundation. The west doorway, by which the tower is entered, is 15th century and above it is a small, round-headed window portraying St Andrew with the X-shaped cross.

From the nave interior can be seen the fine Norman tower arch which is, again, much plainer than the south doorway arch. The only ornamentation is on the pier capitals. There seems to have been a considerable period when there was neither steeple or roof and, whoever rang the bells, had a damp job in bad weather. Deep grooves are to be seen in the stonework of the arch overhead, perhaps caused when the bell was pulled by someone sheltering under the arch.

Surmounting the tower is an octagonal spire, consisting of an oak framework covered with cedar shingles.

The bell chamber contains eight bells, three of which date from 1687. The Church Wardens Book, which commences in 1588, records how, in 1590, the church bells were rung as Elizabeth I passed through Cobham from Stoke, and the ringers had their reward:

> 'Itm layd out to Stydall his wyfe
> For bread and drink sett for the Ringers
> when the Queene went through the
> towne from Mr Lyfelds howse      vijd. (7 d.)
> Itm payd to the Ringers that did
> ring when the Queene went through
> the towne from Mr Lyfields howse      xd. (10 d.)'

The chancel was extended northwards around the year 1200 by the addition of a chantry chapel, which had an altar where masses were sung for the souls of the departed, in accordance with terms laid down at its foundation. Originally almost double its present length, it was truncated during the last century. From the outside the outline of part of one of the original early English lancet windows can be clearly seen. The roof is of Horsham slabs supported by stout oak beams.

Within the chapel are a number of early features. The original triangular-headed double piscina is in the south wall and has two shallow basins and soakaways.

The chapel became the Cobham War Memorial in 1919 and the Italian walnut floor then laid was made from the waste wood of rifle stocks from the First World War. When the old floor was taken up, several fragments of tombstone were found, including parts of a slab of similar date to the Chantry, perhaps part of the founder's tomb.

The stone screen of the chapel was copied from old sculptured work at Worcester Cathedral and the iron work of the arcade is copied from a grille at the Plazzo Communale in Siena.

Between the windows is the memorial roll of the 92 men of Cobham who fell on active service in 1914-18. The names of those who fell in the Second World War are recorded in the books which stand on an oak desk below the original scroll.

At the same time as the building of the Chantry, the chancel was lengthened, the whole being set at a slight angle to the nave. This may be the orientation for sunrise on the festival of St Andrew. The fittings of the chancel, including the altar table and reredos, are comparatively modern. The latter depicts the scene at Emmaus and was presented to the church by Mrs Ethel Combe of Painshill. The clergy and choir stalls were presented in memory of Charles Combe, who died in 1920.

Within the chancel is a magnificent solid brass candelabra made about 1730 and an antique chair, probably late 17th century, which was given to the church in 1838 by William Beckford of Church Stile House — a churchwarden.

Attached to the south wall of the chancel is a small brass plate measuring 6 inches by 4½ inches which is part of a larger composition, the remainder of which is lost. It includes an interesting group of fifteen sons all dressed alike, standing closely together in a row and wearing long contemporary robes. The surviving section of the brass, which dates from about 1500, is almost certainly a unique representation of the Adoration of the Shepherds.

The only other ancient brass to have survived is that attached to the base of the arch near the organ. It is a palimpsest, or double sided brass, and is pivoted so that both sides can be seen. On one side is a figure of a tonsured priest of c1510, wearing eucharistic vestments. He is holding a chalise which bears the inscription ESTO M IHS (ie Esto mihi Jesus) which, freely translated, is 'Be unto me another Jesus'.

On the other side of the brass is a man in armour who is heavily bearded and moustached. He is either George Bigley, who died in 1558, or 'James Sutton sometime Bayle of this Lordshyppe'.

When Chertsey Abbey was dissolved by Henry VIII, the advowson, or right to appoint the incumbent, passed to the King, who then granted it to Bisham Abbey. When that Abbey was dissolved, the right reverted to the Crown and was eventually granted into lay hands and held for a time by the Sutton family, before passing to the Inwoods and then to the Westons. The advowson eventually passed to the Combe family in whose hands it remains.

The first vicar of Cobham, admitted in 1466, was William Clerk. One of his more interesting successors was William King, who was instituted at Cobham in 1626. According to a note in the parish registers in 1644 'Mr King, Vicar of Cobham, did about the begining of Sep. leave this Parish, being afraid lest that he should have been taken by some of the King's party and punished for speaking against His Majesty and justifying the proceedings in Cornwall. And having left the Vicarage he never returned to it again, but was in a short time prepar'd to the Rectory of Asheed' (Ashtead).

John Evelyn heard King at Ashtead in 1658 and recorded in his diary that 'a Quaker would have disputed with him'. King was ejected in 1662 and Samuel Pepys, after a visit to Ashtead Church in 1663, recorded in his diary 'we had a dull Doctor, one Downe, worse than I think ever Parson King was, of whom we have made so much scorn'.

Of the nave of the church, the only old structure to have survived is the roof of collar-trussed oak rafters with plaster, tiled on the outside. Both arcades are nineteenth century, the pillars on the south side being octagonal, those on the north side rounded with capitals in thirteenth century style.

During the nineteenth century, church attendance increased and galleries were erected. When they were removed, every conceivable scrap of space was covered with pews. The Vestry minutes of 30 June 1799 record:

'At a meeting of the Committee appointed to regulate the Pews in the Church, it is ordered that in future all Gentlemen's Livery Servants shall sit in the Gallery, on the south side of the Organ, that all women servants be placed in a pew on the left side next the Gallery and the two opposite ones, and also all women strangers be placed there, and in the next adjoining Pew on the left hand, that all Farmers' servants, apprentices, journeymen and boys and girls sit in the right hand Chancel, the people in the workhouse in the left hand Chancel; that Wm. Watkins be appointed Beadle to attend the inhabitants to their Pews, and that he be provided with a coat and hat, and that each Pew have a Lock fixed as soon as convenient'.

In 1825 the Vestry resolved to 'adopt some method to enlarge the church the same not being large enough to admit the inhabitants to attend Divine Service'. The following year, there was a general re-arrangement of pews and a plan in the Vestry Book shows the new allotments. A subscription list was got up to pay for the re-arrangement and this was headed by HRH Prince Leopold of Claremont, who owned property on the Fairmile in Cobham parish. The sum of £20 was subscribed by the Commissioners of the Navy for a pew allocated 'to the Telegraph', ie (the semaphore tower).

One whole page of the Vestry Book, in 1827, was taken up by a disgruntled Thomas Page, Lord of the Manor, to protest 'against any further alterations or what is called Improvement, in the interior of the said Church'.

The nineteenth century saw a number of 'restorations' and enlargements. In 1853 the south aisle was added and the old windows and door arch from the previous south wall were reused. Victorian glass fills the old windows, most of it of average quality. However, one fortunate addition was the lovely stained glass window over the choir vestry door. This depicts the Annunciation and is from a design by the Pre-Raphaelite artist Sir Edward Burne-Jones. In 1863 alterations were carried out to the north aisle, and it was decided 'that a new chancel arch be built in the place of the present one and that the Chancel be ornamented'. In 1870 it was 'resolved to light the Church with gas'. Further additions and extensions were made in 1872, 1886 and 1902. It is fortunate that the topographical artist Hassell visited the church in the 1820s, to make some water colour sketches, which serve as a record prior to restoration.

45

The organ which now fills the south east corner of the church was presented by Caroline Molesworth of Cobham Lodge, in memory of her mother, and installed in 1850 by Messrs J. W. Walker. It has been enlarged and renovated on several occasions. In 1895 it was played by the young Ralph Vaughan Williams at the marriage of Margaret Lushington of Pyports. The distinguished guests at the wedding of another of Lushington's daughters included Holman Hunt the artist and Julia, wife of Sir Leslie Stephen and mother of Virginia Woolf.

During the course of various restorations a number of the old memorials were removed from their original places in the chancel and some disappeared altogether. At the end of the narrow passage between the clergy vestry and the organ is one of the oldest surviving memorials. Dated 1631, it is in memory of Sarah Coxe, the daughter of a Silkman and Citizen of London. Ralph Cox, in his will is described as 'Saddler'. Above the pillar in the Memorial Chapel there remains one of the old bronze plaques in memory of Aminadab Cooper who died in 1618 'Citizen and Merchant Taylor of London . . . and left behind Dorothy his wife and had issue God-helpe their only son'.

The church register of 1636 records the burial in the chancel of Sir Humphrey Lynde, a well known theologian 'famous for his writing in defence of the Protestant Religion'. No memorial to Sir Humphrey has survived and, strangely, neither are there memorials to the Earl and Countess of Carhampton who were buried here, or the famous Lord Ligonier of Cobham Park who has a monument in Westminster Abbey, although a plaque in memory of Ligonier was placed in the War Memorial Chapel some years ago.

Other monuments have survived: those of Agnes, first wife of Charles Hamilton of Painshill, Thomas Page of Pointers, W.H. Cooper of Painshill and those of various members of the Combe family. There is also a small brass to the memory of Matthew Arnold, the poet who lived in Cobham. In the churchyard are the tombs of Admiral Graham Moore of Brook Farm and Caroline Molesworth of Cobham Lodge. Other tombstones are those of Thomas Tyley who died in 1746 aged 25 and whose epitaph contains a note of urgency:

'Reader Repent and do not delay
For in my Youth I was taken away'.

Near the west door of the tower lies the oddly named Kerenhappuch Jelly and, near the north east corner of the church is the enigma of 'David Archibald — Died 31st February 1880'.

Also in the churchyard is the ancient yew tree in the garden of memory. Yew trees are often found on old sacred sites and this specimen, which is certainly the oldest living thing in Cobham, may even be older than the church.

St John's, the daughter church in Copse Road, was built as a Mission Church in 1899 and was the gift of Miss Carrick Moore of Brook Farm.

LEFT: The interior of St Andrew's by E. Hassell 1827: west end before restoration, and RIGHT: the east end.

46

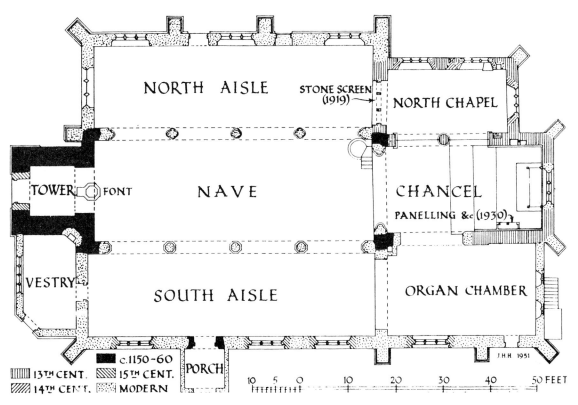

NORTH AISLE

STONE SCREEN (1919)

NORTH CHAPEL

TOWER   FONT

NAVE

CHANCEL

PANELLING &c (1930)

VESTRY

SOUTH AISLE

ORGAN CHAMBER

PORCH

c.1150–60  13TH CENT.  15TH CENT.  14TH CENT.  MODERN

J.H.H. 1951

10  5  0  10  20  30  40  50 FEET

ABOVE: St Andrew's Church: various periods of building and rebuilding;
BELOW: Cobham Church by J. Hassell in 1822.

47

NORMAN DOORWAY     COBHAM CHURCH

LEFT & RIGHT: The palimpsest brass in St Andrew's church — one side shows a man in armour, the other a priest in vestments; CENTRE: The adoration of the shepherds from a brass of c1500 in St Andrew's and a brass formerly there showing a group of fifteen sons. This was probably part of the same one. BELOW: the Norman doorway.

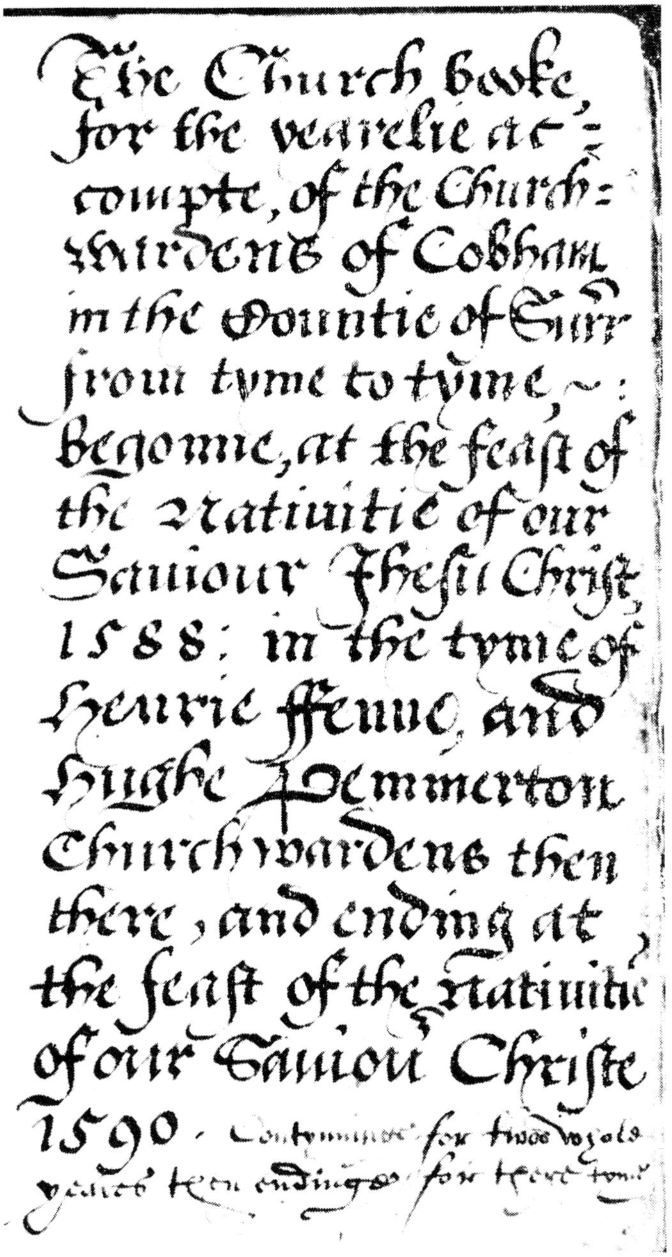

The Church booke,
for the yearelie ac-
compte, of the Church-
wardens of Cobham,
in the Countie of Surr
from tyme to tyme, ~:
begonne, at the feast of
the nativitie of our
Saviour Jhesu Christ,
1588; in the tyme of
Henrie ffenne, and
Hughe Pemmerton
Churchwardens then
there, and ending at
the feast of the nativitie
of our Saviou Christe
1590. Contynninge for twoe wyole
yeares tem endinges for there tone

Title Page of the Churchwardens' Book of 1588.

ABOVE: St Andrew's church in the early nineteenth century, and BELOW: c1905.

50

ABOVE: The Chapel at Cobham Cemetery. LEFT: St Andrew's choir early this century, and RIGHT: the Church Army van in Cobham. The exact location is not known but the photograph was taken by Hugh West of Cobham, the local photographer.

The beginning

*The 20. of the 10th month. 1677*

*At the same meeting friends of Cobham did bring in an account of a peece of ground to build a meeting house upon which may be bought of the Lady Vincent & it was desired by this meeting that they would bring in a full account of the purchase & other Conveniences*

*A subscription for the meeting house in Cobham*

*Agreed at the same meeting that A Subscription be drawn up in order £100 x money for to helpe pay for the building of the meeting house in Cobham & Thomas Inward & George Greethurst to receive the mony of friends one that side, and William Cotterill for Kingston Call this side & when done to bring their accounts to the mens meeting.*

and the end

*It being our mens meeting The Affair of Cobham Meeting house continued Saml Hetherington has not yet Returned the Book Borrows It is agreed at this meeting Between us & Saml Hethering ton That he should have Cobham Meeting house & Ground at the Sume of fifteen pounds The Burial Ground Excepted which is to be fenct of by him & alfo the fence all Round kept in Repair by the Said Saml Hethering & a Sufficient Passage Left to the Burial Ground witness my Hand Saml Hetherington*

*The Mark of Jn Hayman*
*Benj Elgar          Jn Stevens*
*James Hayman        Tho Chandler*
*Joseph Chandlan     Jno Blittle*

Of Cobham Meeting
House

The beginning and the end of Cobham's Quaker Meeting House from the
Minute Book of the Kingston Monthly Meeting.

# Many Causes

The Church of England, established by law in 1539, was intended to create one church. Since some people continued to follow the old ways of Roman Catholicism, while others followed the teachings of Calvin, uniformity was imperfect.

Cobham has had a long and continuous tradition of nonconformity running from at least the seventeenth century to present times. A number of men and women have emerged locally over the past centuries who have felt called by God to write, speak, and practically outwork their faith outside the mainline tradition.

One of Cobham's early 'protesters' was 'Joan Lyster of Cobham Spinster', who, in 1586, was indicted for 'scandalous words' in that she publicly said 'the Bysshop of Canterbury and the Counsayle make fool of the Queens Majestie, and because she is but a woman she ought not to be governer of a Realme. And that the bisshop of Canterbury was but a preest, and that the world wold change erre yt were longe . . .'. Presumably Joan was the sister of George Lyster, the vicar of Cobham who, in 1578, had been indicted for 'failing to wear the surplice during divine service'.

George Fox, the Quaker founder, began his itinerant ministry in 1643, but it was not until some nine years later that the movement began to spread. In 1654 Quakers were active in Kingston upon Thames, some eight miles from Cobham and Fox was there in 1656.

Cobham had become a Quaker centre by the 1670s and a meeting house was built in the village. In 1665 Ephraim Carter, a Cobham butcher, was committed to the White Lyon prison at Southwark for one month for holding meetings in his home. Thomas Barton, a local baker, was also committed for fourteen days. This experience did not discourage Carter, since his name reappears many times in the course of a few years, in connection with the Kingston Meeting House. In 1673 Carter allowed his house, Norwood Farm, to be used for the Quarterly Meeting and he later played a prominent role in the building of the Cobham Meeting House. In that same year of 1673 it was recorded that the Cobham Meeting was attended by 'many of the world's people' — it had clearly become the centre of wide area of Quaker activity. In 1676 a piece of land was purchased and four years later the first Cobham Meeting House was completed at a cost of £7 9s 8d.

During the early years of the eighteenth century, the number of local Quakers appears to have declined, and the last Quarterly Meeting held in Cobham was in 1735. In 1739 the building was sold to Samuel Hetherington for £15. The burial ground was excluded from the sale and not disposed of until the 1840s — for £5. The remaining Cobham Friends had probably long since transferred to the Esher Meeting.

The site of the Cobham Meeting House and its burial ground is uncertain; a deed of 1849 refers to a 'Quaker's Close' at the rear of the site now occupied by the Central Garage on the Portsmouth Road. The Bishop of Winchester's Visitation of 1724-5 recorded that there were then 'no papists here' but 'there is a Quaker meeting. There is one family of Quakers, one of Presbyterians'.

The Independents, or Congregationalists, are known to have met in Cobham during the eighteenth century. In 1764 and 1768 a building near the junction of Downside Road and Plough Lane was registered for worship.

In 1818 a room in the house of Daniel Clarke was registered. The application was signed by William Foster, William Dallen and Edward Trigg. Trigg, a local hairdresser, had been converted under a visiting street preacher. A short biography of Trigg, written by a friend shortly after his death, states that he left part of his estate towards the building of a chapel in the village. The evangelist responsible for Trigg's conversion may well have been the unusual Strict Baptist Minister, William Huntingdon of Thames Ditton. Huntingdon had become minister of Providence Chapel, Woking, in 1776 and later extended his ministry to a number of nearby villages including Cobham. During his latter years, Huntingdon adopted the style 'William Huntingdon S.S.' (Sinner Saved) and even had this painted on the side of his carriage.

A life of Huntingdon is inscribed as a gift to the former Ebenezer Strict Baptist Chapel at Cobham 'which was one of the many causes founded by William Huntingdon'. The chapel, now a youth club, was opened in 1873 on land given by a local Strict Baptist pastor, Edgar Hewlett.

In 1824, John R. Gayton was one of the signatories to an application to register a meeting house which was 'an outbuilding of which Giles Notley is occupier at Street Cobham'. Gayton was an agent of the Surrey Mission and had commenced evangelistic work in Cobham in 1821 and, in 1822, Giles Notley occupied part of the George Inn at Street Cobham.

The Independents were next recorded in 1847 when Miss Mellor of Downside, concerned at the spiritual state of the neighbourhood and what she called 'the sports and heathenish pastimes' that took place on Downside Common on Sundays, opened her home for meetings. At the first meeting on 2 April 1848, considerable disturbance was caused by some local youngsters, who got into the room and began to let off fireworks. The clubroom behind the George Inn was still used for meetings and as a temporary place of worship until a chapel was built nearby in 1854, on the site now occupied by Alsford's timber yard. The chapel remained in use until the early part of this century, when it was closed down and demolished. A new Congregational Church (now the United Reformed Church) was opened in Stoke Road.

John Wesley, founder of the Methodist Church, had been to Cobham on a number of occasions, though apparently never to preach. His object was to visit the famous gardens at Painshill. Methodism was not to have any real impact on the district until the middle of the nineteenth century. Wesleyan home missionaries had been active in the area in the early years of the last century and were, for a while, supervised by the famous missionary Thomas Coke.

In the late 1850s, Samuel Wesley Bradnack, with his wife Juliana, moved to the Cedars (now Pyports) in Church Street. Samuel was the son of a well known Wesleyan missionary, Isaac Bradnack, and had moved to Cobham from Ipswich, where he ran a small private boarding school. The school moved with him to Cobham and he advertised vacancies in the *Methodist Recorder,* with fees of sixty guineas per annum.

At this time Cobham's great downfall seems to have been the demon drink and a visiting nonconformist minister thought that Cobham was 'as dark as heathendom itself', and that 'the teaching of the clergy is cold and semi papistical'.

Prompted by the spiritual state of the village, Bradnack hired a cottage in Downside to reach what he called 'the baptised heathens' of the district. His congregation grew and he opened his home for meetings. Evenutally the old barn at Pyports was fitted up as a place of worship and students from the Richmond Theological College came to preach there. One of the great Methodist divines of the period, Thomas Jackson, was also a frequent visitor to Cobham.

This was the time of the great 1859 revival which spread from the USA to Ulster, and then across to England, producing great Christians like Dr Barnardo, James Chalmers and Hugh Price Hughes. One observer of the Ulster revival was Benjamin Scott of Weybridge and he probably first sparked the Cobham revival. There are stirring accounts in contemporary religious periodicals of the meetings in the barn at Pyports, of changed lives and of drunkards finding peace with God. The movement spread from Cobham and preaching centres were set up in Ripley, Ockham, Oxshott, Horsley and other nearby villages. However, as revival spread, so did opposition — particularly from the established church, which eventually forced Bradnack to leave, first The Cedars, and then Cobham. In 1862, the local schoolmaster had burned a copy of the Wesleyan catechism before the whole school, to show his contempt for the movement, and a certain 'good woman', on telling the vicar that she followed the Methodists, was told 'Then they will lead you to the Devil. The doctrine of assurance is a doctrine of the devils'.

From The Cedars, Bradnack and his school moved to Lime House, Church Street, and a cottage in the High Street was used as a meeting place. Eventually land for a chapel was purchased in Cedar Road and the building opened in April 1862. For a short period, the Methodists held meetings in a large tent on land near Pyports, possibly the Leg Of Mutton Field, and here 'a remarkable outpouring of the Holy Spirit' took place.

Bradnack, his family, and school moved to Surbiton and then to Folkstone. At Surbiton, a pupil at the school was Thomas Anstey Guthrie, who later became a well known writer. His novel *Vice Versa* parodied life at the school and Bradnack was caricatured as the formidable 'Dr. Grimstone'.

The original Methodist Church in Cedar Road was demolished in 1966 and the former Sunday School building was adopted as the new church.

The Plymouth, or Christian Brethren have been active in Cobham since the early part of the century, and have a Gospel Hall in Anyards Road.

Members of the Roman Catholic Church met in various homes in Cobham during the nineteenth century and, in 1912, Holly Lodge (a building formerly in the High Street) became the home of Cobham's first resident priest. In 1915 Spencer House (now Ham Manor) was acquired with the hope that it would become a home for an order of Brigittine Priests. Roman Catholics continued to meet in an outbuilding of Ham Manor and in a room at the former Royal Oak public house on the Portsmouth Road. In 1930, a temporary church was built in Cedar Road and replaced a few years later by the building which now houses a nursery school. The present Roman Catholic Church was built in Between Streets to the designs of H.S. Goodhart-Rendel in 1957 and is probably the most attractive of all Cobham's new buildings.

More recently a group known locally as the Cobham Fellowship has made its mark on the community in a similar manner to the early Quakers, Independents and Methodists. A fresh approach to worship and a radical Christian life-style in which the gifts of the Holy Spirit, as recorded in the New Testament, have an important role, are some of the hallmarks of the group. One of the group's leaders, Gerald Coates, is now well known throughout the country as a Christian preacher and teacher, and Cobham has become a centre for many involved in what has been termed the Charismatic Movement. A feature of recent years has been the Kingdom Life Meetings held in a large marquee on the Leg Of Mutton Field, in the footsteps of Samuel Bradnack and the early Methodists.

ABOVE LEFT: William Huntington S.S. the Strict Baptist Minister who helped found Cobham's Baptist Chapel in Cedar Road. RIGHT: Norwood Farm, home of Ephraim Carter, the Cobham Quaker. BELOW: The old Congregational Chapel at Street Cobham which stood on the site now occupied by Alsford's Timber Yard. RIGHT: Cobham's first Methodist Chapel opened in Cedar Road in 1862 and demolished in 1964.

Cobham Methodist Sunday School

### Annual
# Summer Outing
to be held on
## Friday, July 7th, 1939
## To LITTLEHAMPTON
Starting Point: General Post Office
High Street          Time: 7 a.m.

*Adult*           *Fare 5/6*

ABOVE: Cobham Methodist Sunday School Annual Summer Outing 1939;
CENTRE '1860 — Presented to S.W. Bradnack Esq. by the Inhabitants of
Cobham as a Testimonial of their regard & esteem for his Christian Virtues
and true Philantrophy (sic).' Now in the possession of Miss B.M. Bradnack of
Felixstowe. RIGHT: Samuel Wesley Bradnack and his wife Juliana;
BELOW: The 'Kingdom Life' tent on the Leg Of Mutton Field.

57

# The True
# Levellers Standard

*ADVANCED:*

OR,

The State of Community opened, and Presented to the
Sons of Men.

By

William Everard,
Iohn Palmer,
Iohn South,
Iohn Courton.
William Taylor,
Christopher Clifford,
Iohn Barker.

Ferrard Winstanley,
Richard Goodgroome,
Thomas Starre,
William Hoggrill,
Robert Sawyer,
Thomas Eder,
Henry Bickerstaffe,
Iohn Taylor, &c.

Beginning to Plant and Manure the Waste land upon
George-Hill, in the Parish of Walton, in the
County of Surrey.

*Aprill 26*

*LONDON,*
Printed in the Yeer, MDCXLIX.

Title page from 'The True Levellers Standard Advanced' 1649, showing the
names of Winstanley, Everard and several other members of the Digger
community.

# A Common Treasury

Seventeenth century Cobham touched briefly on the nation's affairs. The civil war had resulted in the breakdown of political controls, censorship and church courts. Free discussion followed on many previously unmentionable subjects such as democracy, equality, communism and the abolition of aristocracy and the state church. The Bible became the source of all wisdom and many preachers and teachers emerged with their own individualistic interpretation of current events. One such man was Gerrard Winstanley, a native of Wigan who later moved down to London as a clothing apprentice. In 1640 Winstanley appears to have married Susan King, the daughter of a Cobham family.

Winstanley ran into financial difficulties and left London for Surrey. In 1649 he was herding cows for his neighbours in the vicinity of Cobham and Walton on Thames. It was perhaps as a result of this personal misfortune that he experienced intense soul-searching and felt divinely called to break the 'Norman Yoke' imposed on this country in 1066 and to treat 'the earth as a common treasury for all'. Politically, Winstanley is now hailed by many as the true father of English Socialism, and certainly his writings give clear guide lines for a Utopian socialist state that was way ahead of his time. Others before Winstanley had committed to paper their ideas for the perfect state but none had been prepared to take his brave step of turning word into action.

In fulfillment of that divine commission, given to him during the course of meditation, Winstanley gathered about him a small group of followers who became known as Diggers or True Levellers and these people set about clearing and planting common land on St George's Hill near Cobham. Their actions brought them into conflict with the local lords of the manors who effectively controlled the common land. A petition was sent by the land owners to the Council of State, and the Commander in Chief of the Army, General Thomas, Lord Fairfax, was asked to investigate this 'great number of persons gathered together about Cobham in a tumultuous and riotous manner'.

Fairfax's representative, Captain Gladman, came to Cobham ready to fight but on arrival his assessment of the situation was that 'the business was not worth the writing or taking notice of'. However it was arranged for both Winstanley, and his assistant William Everard, to appear before Fairfax the next day in a famous scene, when both Diggers refused to remove their hats in the presence of the General who they considered was 'but their fellow creature'. They explained their plans and convinced Fairfax that they meant no harm. Any rights in the commons claimed by the lords of the manors had, Winstanley explained, been 'cut off with the King's head'. The General was sympathetic and let them go with a warning.

Fairfax later visited the Digger colony and was moderately impressed by what he saw. Despite the fact that there had been a number of skirmishes with local people, he considered the Diggers constituted no real threat to the central government, and thought that they could be left to the mercy of the local justices.

One of the principal antagonists was Parson John Platt, Lord of the Manor of Cobham and Rector of West Horsley. Another was Francis Drake of Walton on Thames, who brought an action for trespass against the Diggers in the court at Kingston upon Thames. The Diggers asked to be heard in their own defence, being both unwilling on principle, and financially unable to retain their own lawyer, but this plea was dismissed and a hostile jury found against them. As they were unable to pay the fines and costs their goods and cattle were carried off by the bailiffs.

Local opposition, stirred up by Platt and other local landowners, continued. At a meeting held in the White Lion at Cobham when 'a great deal of sack and tobacco was consumed', local traders were persuaded to boycott the Diggers.

The Diggers eventually left St George's Hill and moved to the Little Heath between Cobham and Oxshott and here, in 1650, eleven acres of corn and half a dozen temporary houses were destroyed in a bloody action. Shortly before this event two emmissaries were sent out by the Cobham Diggers to similar colonies that had by now been established in other parts of the Home Counties. With them went a letter signed by Winstanley and twenty one others asking for financial support, but it was too late. The Cobham community appears to have come to an end by Easter 1650, when Winstanley and fourteen other Diggers were indicted for disorderly and unlawful assembly.

Little is known of the fate of the individual Diggers. Many of their names are known from the published tracts and petitions of Winstanley. In 1650 Winstanley and some of his 'poor bretheren' hired themselves to Lady Eleanor Davies at Pireton, Herts. Lady Eleanor was an eccentric personality who believed that she had the gift of prophecy. In December of 1650, Winstanley had cause to write to her ladyship to complain of her failure to pay him and his group.

Winstanley's later life remains something of a mystery, although recent research indicates that he came back to Cobham for a while before returning to London where he died.

Gerrard Winstanley's first wife Susan was the daughter of William King who owned a property called Stewards Mead in the manor of Ham in Cobham. He turned over other property, which he purchased from the Smith family, to the use of his daughter and her husband and made provision in his will that it was to pass to Winstanley's heirs if he and Susan should have no children. Susan's early death meant that Winstanley became once more a man of property and he is listed among the tenants of Ham in 1662. His name is found in the Cobham parish records as both a Churchwarden and an Overseer of the Poor. The registers also record the baptisms of three of his children between 1665 and 1669. In 1671 and 1672 he is recorded as one of two Chief Constables of the Elmbridge Hundred.

This apparent prosperity and rejection of his earlier radical activities may have triggered the criticism levelled at Winstanley by preacher Lawrence Clarkson in 1660, when he wrote of his 'most shameful retreat from George's Hill, with a spirit of pretended universality, to become a real Tithe-gatherer of propriety'.

A Gerrard Winstanley who died a Quaker in London in 1676 may well have been the same man as the Cobham Digger, particularly as Winstanley the Digger had links with the Quakers in Kingston upon Thames in 1647. Many writers have commented that the Diggers came from areas where Quakers were numerous and that much of Winstanely's writing seems to reflect the Quaker influence.

The Diggers were virtually forgotten for two centuries to all but a few historians. However, modern politics have once more brought Winstanley into the limelight and a great many books and learned articles have been published about both man and message. The episode has also been featured on television and radio as well as in a full length film: *Winstanley*.

OPPOSITE : Title page from 'A Declaration to the Powers of England' 1649; INSET: Sir Thomas Fairfax — Commander in Chief of Cromwell's Army.

Robert Coster, the Digger poet, wrote these lines from The Diggers' Song:

'You noble diggers all, stand up now, stand up now,
You noble diggers all, stand up now.
The waste land to maintain seeing cavaliers by name,
And persons all defame,
Stand up now, stand up now.
Your houses they pull down, stand up now, stand up now,
Your houses they pull down, stand up now.
Your houses they pull down, to fright poor men in town,
But the gentry must come down, and the poor shall wear the crown,
Stand up now, Diggers all.'

A
# DECLARATION
TO THE
## Powers of England,
AND

To all the Powers of the VVorld, shewing the
Cause why the common People of England have be-
gun, and gives consent to dig up, manure, and sow Corn upon George-Hill in Surrey; by those that have subscribed, and
thousands more that give consent.

O R,

The state of Community opened, and presented to the Sons of Men.

BY

| William Everard, | Christopher Clifford, | William Hoggrill, |
| John Palmer, | John Barker, | Robert Sawyer, |
| John South, | Ferrard Winstanley, | Thomas Eder, |
| John Courton, | Richard Goodgroom, | Henry Bickerstaffe, |
| William Taylor, | Thomas Starre, | John Taylor, &c. |

Beginning to plant, and manure the wast Land upon George-Hill,
neare Walton, in the County of Surrey.

LONDON,
Printed for Giles Calvert, at the Black Spread-Eagle at the
West end of Pauls. 1649.

# AN
# APPEAL
To the Houſe of
# COMMONS,

Deſiring their A N S VV E R :

VVhether the Common - people
ſhall have the quiet enjoyment of the
*Commons* and *Waſte Land;*

Or whether they ſhall be under the will of
*Lords* of *Mannors* ſtill.

Occaſioned by an Arreſt, made by *Thomas* Lord
*Wenman, Ralph Verny* Knight, and *Richard Winwood* Eſq;
upon the Author hereof, for a Treſpaſs, in D gging
upon the Common-Land at *Georges* Hill in *Surrey.*

By *Gerrard Winſtanly, Iohn Barker,* and *Thomas
Star,* In the Name of all the poor oppreſſed
in the Land of *E N G L A N D.*

*Unrighteous Oppreſſion kindles a flame; but Love, Righteouſ-
neſs, and Tenderneſs of heart, quenches it again.*

## Printed in the Year, 1649.

Title page from 'An Appeal To The House Of Commons' 1649. Written by
Winstanley, Barker and Star.

The Diggers clearing the land, from the film *Winstanley*.

LEFT: Edward I from a contemporary document; he visited Down Place
between 1292 and 1306; CENTRE: the arms of the Downe family, and
RIGHT: Lord Ligonier of Cobham Park; BELOW: the former Cobham Park
from a drawing of c1820 (entrance front).

64

# Cobham Park

Most English towns and villages traditionally have their 'big house' around which the life of the local community has revolved for centuries, and Cobham is no exception. The present Cobham Park, which stands hidden from public view on the Downside Road, is the successor to a number of houses that have stood here for at least eight hundred years. Although never the manor house, Cobham Park has always been the most important estate and the Combe family, who came here in the early 19th century, became local squires and probably played a more important part in local affairs than the lords of the manor, who lived away from Cobham.

Cobham Park was formerly Downe Place, the name suggested by the hill or down which rises steeply from the river, and which can be seen clearly across the Mole from Tilt Road. The name Cobham Park was adopted in the last century and was formerly the name for Downside Common. This was an open space which, by grant of Henry I, the Abbot of Chertsey could enclose when he wished for hunting foxes, hares, pheasants and wild cats.

In the reign of King John, a certain Deodonatus de Dunes held land in Cobham and presumably lived at Downe Place. Later a William de la Dune held the Royal office of Keeper of the Hanaper and was responsible for receiving the money paid for the use of the King's seal. State documents of Edward I, dated at Cobham, indicate Royal visits to Cobham Park between 1292 and 1306. The estate was then leased out by Chertsey Abbey and, in 1331, the death of William de Doune and the admission of his son Henry as tenant, involved payment to the Abbey of an ox, nine gallons of honey, and a horse when required, to take a monk to ordination. Henry was succeeded by his son John.

John a Downe, King's Servant, was MP for Guildford in 1449-50. In 1565 at Croydon Assizes, a certain Joan Gowse was indicted for witchcraft. It was claimed that on 1 December 1564, at Cobham, she bewitched to death an ox belonging to James Adowne.

In 1598 Thomas Adoune was at Downe Place and probably a member of the inquest jury in Cobham in 1568 which found Elizabeth Colpitt guilty of murdering her illegitimate daughter in the house of William Stone, a Cobham innholder. She put her into a saw pit near the house and smothered her in sawdust. In 1607 Thomas Adoune died leaving £2 to the vicar for sermons on Christmas Day and Ash Wednesday, and 20s to the poor, to be given in good bread in church on Ash Wednesday, after the sermon.

In 1671 'Downe hall alias Downe place' was the property of George Smyther who, in that year, settled the property on himself, his wife Anne and his heirs. George was the nephew of John Downe, thus continuing that family's unbroken link with the estate. In 1702 the Cobham parish registers record John Smyther of Dorking as owner, and a deed of 1703 mentions Anne Smyther, widow, and her daughters Elizabeth and Jane. On 13 October 1720 'the capital messuage called Downe place alias Downe hall and all Barnes lands belonging — containing 140 acres in Cobham and Little Bookham Common Surrey in Tenure of John Box' were conveyed to Frances, Viscountess Lanesborough and a letter of that year from her solicitor stated that 'she had found greate benefitt by the country ayre and that her health is much improved'. In fact, Lady Lanesborough died the following year, leaving both the manor of Cobham, and Downe Place to her grandsons of the Fox family. In 1728 Lady Lanesborough's title to the Cobham estate was examined when a commission met at Dorking. They were looking into the mental state of Elizabeth Smyther, as her cousin John Tamworth had sued for a Commission of Idiocy against her.

The house was rebuilt in the classical style in the early eighteenth century by John Bridges. Defoe's *A Tour Through The Whole Island of Great Britain* gives a description:

'The Appartments within seem very commodius, and the principal rooms are elegantly fitted up, the ceilings being gilt, and all the Members are richly ornamented. The Offices below are very conveniently and judiciously contrived to answer the purposes for which they were designed. But what chiefly struck my Curiosity on seeing it was a false Storey contrived on each side of the House, taken from the Difference in the Height of the side-rooms, from those Principal Apartments; and these are converted into long galleries with a small Appartment at one end, which affords a communication between them. In the Attick Story there are very good Lodging-rooms, which are well laid together: so that for the size of this House, there is hardly any other near London, which has more useful and elegant Apartments'.

The account continues with a description of the grounds, which had been partially landscaped (perhaps in imitation of the park at nearby Painshill). Bridges had widened the river in places and the excavated soil used to create 'a natural slope, with a broad Grass-walk, planted with sweet Shrubs on each side; and at the End of the Walk is a fine Room, which has a view of the Water lengthwise, and is a sweet retreat in hot weather'. The house was based on Palladio's designs for his Villa Zeno.

In the middle of the eighteenth century, the estate was purchased by John, Viscount Ligonier, a colourful military man of Huguenot descent. Born in Provence, Ligonier had fought under Marlborough at Blenheim and subsequently rose to become Commander in Chief of the British Army in 1757. He took part in no less than twenty-three general actions and nineteen sieges without receiving a wound. His guests at Cobham included William Pitt the elder and, while the house was chiefly a place of retreat and leisure, in 1759 it was used as his headquarters when laying out the camp on Send Heath near Woking.

It is alleged that Ligonier kept a harem at Cobham of four young girls, and to have said that no woman past the age of fourteen was worth the trouble of pursuing. The combined ages of his four mistresses did not exceed fifty eight years!

Ligonier died in 1770, aged 89, and his monument was erected in Westminster Abbey. He was buried in Cobham Church. The Earl was succeeded by his nephew Edward who, in the following year, divorced his wife Penelope after fighting a sword duel in Hyde Park with her lover, Count Alfieri, an Italian poet. It seems that Lady Ligonier had a reputation that matched that of her husband's late uncle and she was described as a classic example of depravity. It was written of her that she was 'a Lady so Dove-like in the Temper of her Constitution, that she granted without the Preliminaries of Entreatry, every Indulgence which the most lawless inclination could suggest'. Count Alfieri once climbed into Cobham Park to visit his mistress.

After Edward's death in 1782, the estate was sold to General Henry Lawes Luttrell, 2nd Earl of Carhampton and Colonel of the 6th Regiment of Dragoon Guards. His wife Jane was considered to be one of the most beautiful women of her time.

A Land Tax Receipt of 1 March 1800 states that 'the Mansion House and Pleasure Grounds; The Park, Canal, Meadows and Trusslers Field; The new allotments in the late enclosure; The farm etc.' were all then in the occupation of Alexander Raby, the Downside Ironmaster. Raby seems to have occupied various houses in the area, including Stoke Manor House.

Lord Carhampton moved to Painshill in 1804. A coloured glass window containing the Carhampton crest, is all that survives from their time at the house.

In 1806 Downe Place, as it was still known, was purchased by Harvey Christian Combe for the sum of £30,000. Combe, a brewer and friend of both the Prince of Wales and Charles James Fox, had been Lord Mayor of London in 1799 and MP for the City in 1802.

He continued the policy of enlarging and improving the park, and a bill of 1807, from his lawyer, refers to work done in connection with 'Having two Publick Highways in your Grounds diverted and turned thro' other parts thereof and a footpath stopped up'. The road was the approach to Downside Mill and Farm. Two years later, John Balchin, Parish Surveyor of the Highways acknowledged receipt of £15 4s for the purchase of the old highway.

In 1812 Harvey Combe served on a Drury Lane Theatre Committee. Five years later he resigned all such offices following an insult, and in July 1818 died at Cobham, having suffered from paralysis for many years. He left an estate worth £200,000. The stables at the Park, which are older than the present house, contain an inscribed tablet from the old Woodyard Brewhouse in London, dated 1848. The figure of a fox on the side of the stable block is also said to have come from London.

Harvey Combe was succeeded by his son, also named Harvey, one time Master of the Old Berkley Hunt, who had a locomotive named after him. The *Harvey Combe* was the 123rd engine made by Robert Stephenson & Co, and was used in 1836-7 in the construction of the London and Birmingham Railway near Berkhampstead. The second Harvey's death in 1857 was followed by a sale of his Shorthorn cattle at Downside Farm, which raised upwards of £5,000.

By now the house had acquired its present name, and Brayley's *History of Surrey,* published in the early nineteenth century, described it as 'a handsome and substantial building, nearly square, with a neat portico erected in the place of a verandah. The good saloon, with coved and ornamented ceiling, was turned into a billiard room, and the other convenient apartments were embellished with busts and pictures'. But as the *Monthly Magazine* of 1834 remarked:

'Let lofty mansions great men keep —
I have no wish to rob 'em —
Not courtly Claremont, Esher's steep,
Nor Squire Combe's at Cobham.'

Combe family drawings suggest an enlargement of the house was considered — a new wing on either side. However, a fire precipitated rebuilding in its entirety in the early 1870s. Once a broken headstone stood in Cobham churchyard, in memory of two workmen killed by a fall from scaffolding in 1871.

The new house, completed in 1873, is built of Bargate and Portland stone to the designs of Edward Middleton Barry RA, third son of Sir Charles Barry, architect of the Palace of Westminster and the nearby Charing Cross Hotel. Only the cellars and basement area of the previous house remain, although architectural features from the building have been found scattered around the grounds.

Built at a cost of £26,000 by Charles Combe, Cobham Park is reputed to have been the third house in the country to have electricity, a generator wheel having been installed at Downside Mill (purchased by Combe in 1865 for £3,150). Another small wheel was installed in the Park by Whitmore and Binyon of Wickham Market, Suffolk, in 1884, to bring water to the house. Elsewhere in the grounds is an ice house in the hillside. The ice house was filled with ice from the lake in the winter and, when packed with straw, it lasted throughout the summer.

Charles Combe was Harvey Combe junior's nephew, born in 1836. He served in the Third Bombay Cavalry in Persia and in the Indian Mutiny. Throughout the last half of the last century Cobham Park remained central to Cobham affairs. Charles Combe's uncle supplied the people of Downside with water in 1858 and the schools in Cedar Road were erected by Miss Combe in 1860.

Charles Combe had tried to bring the railway here in the 1860s. He was questioned by a select committee of the House of Lords and when one commented 'Yours is a very nice estate at Cobham and a very convenient mansion house', Combe replied 'It is not a convenient house because I am going to pull it down'. Combe's philanthropic works led to Cobham's first volunteer fire service, the provision of a village hall and the creation of Cobham Cemetery.

Most of the original decoration of the house remains and, in the entrance hall, the large oak mantlepiece is enriched by a square panel carved with the Combe coat of arms, impaling Inglis (Mrs Combe's family), three lions, one rampant, and three stars. The two heads on either side of the fireplace appear to represent Charles Combe and his wife in mediaeval attire. The house formerly contained a number of family portraits and marble statues of members of the family, by the Victorian sculptor Williamson, who lived in Esher.

Visitors to Squire Combe and his family at the Park would have included Matthew Arnold, a Cobham resident. Charles Combe witnessed at the marriage of Arnold's daughter in 1884. Another visitor was Rosa Lewis, the 'Duches of Duke Street', a friend of the valet.

The routine orderliness of life in a typical country house was disturbed in 1925 when Duncan McKenzie, Charles Combe's butler, committed suicide with his master's revolver.

The Combe family gave up Cobham Park as a family residence in the 1930s, Charles Combe having moved to Painshill in 1904 following Lord Carhampton. In 1939, imminent war brought the Eagle Star Insurance Group from London to the Cobham area. Cobham Park became their administrative centre and they remained until 1958. During the war years, the squash courts at the Park were converted into a Club with table tennis, darts, bar billiards and full size billiard table. Monthly dances were arranged for staff, members of the armed forces and local people.

The house is now occupied by Logica, a high technology company specialising in computing science, communications, office automation and management sciences. Since it moved to Cobham Park in 1979, the company has carried out an extensive scheme of restoration and redecoration.

The former Cobham Park from a drawing of c1820 (garden front).

ABOVE: 'English Patriots Bowing At The Shrine Of Despotism': a satirical comment by Gilray on the visit to Napoleon by Fox, Erskine and Harvey Combe, and BELOW: the present Cobham Park, from a late nineteenth century photo.

ABOVE: Charles Combe, the builder of the present Cobham Park, with his
first wife and family, and BELOW: the conservatory at Cobham Park, c1890.

ABOVE: The entrance to Cobham Park; LEFT: Charles Harvey Combe —
MP for the Chertsey Division of Surrey 1892-1897, and RIGHT:
gamekeeper at Cobham Park (c1890).

Charles Combe Esqre

To    Holland & Hannen

For Works done in erecting the Mansion at
Cobham Park.

                              Edward M. Barry Esqre R.A.
May 1874.                        Architect

                                               £  s  d

To Amount of Contract for the Mansion  28,170. 0. 0

New Woodhouse with walls and balustrade
    connected therewith _____     512. 1. 10

Extra on Kitchen offices in consequence
    of change of site of Mansion
    including additional parapets
    balustrades, increased size of larder   258. 0. 0
    tile linings to walls of do, additional
    doors, ventilating flues &c _____

Lowering ground line of North and
    part of East front including extra   405. 14. 3.
    steps to Library window_____

Area to kitchen Offices West front      63. 8. 0

Extra on part of Ground floor being
    made fireproof _____          305. 11. 6.
                        Contd £29714. 15. 7.

Extract from architect's bill for Cobham Park.

72

ABOVE: Extract of plan showing proposed garden lay out at Cobham Park.
BELOW: The Eagle Star at Cobham Park — the staff dining hall.

ABOVE: Cobham Mill 1809 and the road in front of Cedar House and the mill building – demolished in 1953. The present mill was not built until about 1820. BELOW: Cobham Mill by J. Hassell 1822; in the background, Leigh Hill House, later the Leigh Place Hotel.

74

# Mills on the Mole

Cobham's best known landmark is the red brick water mill which now stands silently by the river Mole. The present building, locally known as 'the old mill', was built about one hundred and sixty years ago, and is only part of a once larger complex.

Before 1850, half the population of England lived in agricultural settings, and grain milling was a vital industry throughout the arable lowlands. Watermills were introduced by the Romans, and Domesday records many mills, which were then an important capital asset, including three at Cobham. These were Cobham and Downside Mills and a mill near Ash Ford on Cobham Tilt. The steep gradient of the river Mole at Cobham, where it falls about seven feet in half a mile, makes this an excellent site.

Ashford mill, mentioned as one of the bounds of Cobham in the Cartulary of Chertsey Abbey, had disappeared by 1598 when Ralph Agas made his survey of the manor. However, the tithe map of 1845 shows Mill field and Mill meadow on the site of the present Cobham cemetery.

Cobham Mill was leased from the Abbot of Chertsey in 1534 by Richard Sutton, and a survey of 1546-9 refers to the King's mill called 'stewarde mill', and also to 'Coveham myll' in the tenure of John Collyn. The former, then in the tenure of Thomas Tailler, belonged to the manor of Ham and possibly adjoined Cobham Mill.

Edward VI granted Cobham Mill to Sir Anthony Browne in 1552 for a term of 21 years on the condition that Browne should repair the 'Cogges, Ronges, and les Bayes of the said Mill'. In 1552, George Bygley, gentleman and servant of Sir Anthony Browne, demised the mill to Thomas Howse and, in 1572, Robert Gavell and Dorothy his wife, son-in-law and daughter of George Bygley, demised the mill to William Sewer of Fetcham, the premises then described as one corn mill and one malt mill 'being under one roofe'.

In the 1770s Alice Fairfax Lucy's history of the Lucy family of Charlecote, Warwickshire, records that a man calling himself Thomas Lucy travelled from Cobham to Charlecote to put forward a claim for a large landed property. Thomas Lucy said that he bought Cobham Mill, and an action had been brought against him for fishing in the Mole. He won but his legal expenses were so heavy that he was obliged to sell the mill. He believed that through his pedigree he was related to the Warwickshire family and thereby had a claim on the estate. George Lucy of Charlecote was apparently so impressed by the evidence that he proposed to settle money on Thomas so he could set himself up with other premises.

Thomas Lucy appears to have had a dispute with the local Vestry as to the amount of Poor Rate levied on his premises in February 1784. The Vestry recorded that 'whereas a council has been applied to concerning raising Mr. Lucy's Taxes and the said Council's opinion is that it cannot be done — and whereas Mr. Lucy now refuses to pay his original Rates, it is hereby agreed that he be compell's thereto by Law'. However, by June of the same year, Lucy's house, mill and meadow were assessed at £30 per annum from Michaelmas 1783 and it was also agreed 'to give Mr. Lucy Five Pounds towards his expenses in his late Law suit concerning his Rates'.

A lease of the mill to Thomas Lucy is dated 1777 and his name is also to be found in connection with The Old Mill House which stands across the road from the mill. This mediaeval hall house was traditionally the miller's home. In Georgian times the building was refronted in brick and over the door is a Sun fire mark from whose number the following details have been traced:

'30th September 1779 £

THOMAS LUCY of Cobham in Surrey Miller on his new dwelling house only

| | |
|---|---:|
| situate as aforesaid not exceeding Two Hundred Pounds | 200 |
| Stock and Goods therein not exceeding Fift Pounds | 50 |
| Water Corn Mill with the going Gear not exceeding Four Hundred Pounds | 400 |
| Utensils and Stock not exceeding One Hundred and Ninety Pounds | 190 |
| Barns Stables and Carthouses adjoining not exceeding One Hundred and Fifty Pounds | 150 |
| Utensils and Stock thereunto only not exceeding One Hundred Pounds | 100 |
| Stock within Open Yard not exceeding Ten Pounds | 10 |

all Brick Timber and Tiles

G. Mason          J. Watts          N. Pearce                                              '

Thomas Lucy remained at the mill until 1787, when he was succeeded by John Tupper, who stayed until 1803. In 1799 the mill was severely damaged by flooding and assistance was sought by means of a nationally proclaimed church brief. In 1803 James Peto, meal merchant and miller took a lease. Deeds held by the Combe family suggest that the mill was held under a deed of settlement for a large part of the nineteenth century.

The topographical writer and artist John Hassell has left us a water colour of the mill as it appeared in 1822 and, for at least one hundred years, Cobham Mill has been a favourite subject for artists.

In 1861 the barrister and poet A.J. Munby passed through Cobham and recorded in his journal:

'The old fashioned mill with a large undershot wheel in full play and then comes the mill race, a long quiet strip of water broadening out beyond the weir into a pretty view with old red houses on one side and willows on the other, and the church spire in the midst'.

The artist Roddam Spencer Stanhope, who lived at Cobham then, painted this same view, suitably embellished with a Pre-Raphaelite maiden languishing in a punt in the foreground.

In 1871 Mrs Batchelor was the 'Master Miller employing five men and one boy' here. Her nephew Thomas Sweetlove took a lease of the mill in 1890 for 21 years. Two years later, *Cobham Parish Magazine* reported:

'The road by the river which has long been a disgrace to our village is at length being improved; and we are promised that when it is completed we shall never run the risk of having more than a foot or two of water through which to wade or drive in our passage to and from the station'.

This section of the road still remains liable to seasonal floods, the worst in living memory being in 1968.

Henry Moore and Son later purchased the mill and Cobham authoress Mrs Earle in *A Third Pot-Pouri From A Surrey Garden* commends the firm's various flours and fresh bran. A tragedy occured there in 1912 when Harold Lynn, who the *Parish Magazine* described as 'one of the most deservedly popular and promising young men of the village' was accidentally killed while assisting workmen to repair the wheels. Moore and Son sold the mill to C.H. Combe in 1925 and the present owners are Surrey County Council. They have leased it to a private tenant for restoration.

The mill in fact closed in the late 1920s. In 1926 a report in the *Surrey Comet* confidently stated that: 'there is no danger, we understand, of the old mill either being destroyed or becoming altogether derelict. The reason for the present stoppage is that Messrs. H. Moore and Son who have been millers there for many years, are not renewing the lease ... Much of the exterior of the present mill, a feature of which is the sharp gables, is comparatively modern, but the interior stones and woodwork certainly indicate considerable age. The main support is a venerable oak pile — practically a whole tree trunk, some four feet in diameter at the base... This wheel is one of the widest in the country, and is capable of producing 30 horse power. The smaller wheel is of metal and is more modern, and attains about 12 horse power. When working at full pressure the mill has ground as much as three tons of flour a day. Lately, it has only been used for grinding pig and poultry food'.

Concern for the preservation of the mill has often been expressed, more lately by the Cobham Conservation Group. In 1931 it was the subject of a report in the *Times* following planning proposals criticised for not providing a riverside walk or suitable treatment for the setting.

Henry Wren of Oxshott wrote to the *Times* suggesting that 'Cobham should, in laying out a surround for this minor national possession — provide something in the nature of a riverside amenity as well as mere sports grounds to be used by young folk'. This was followed by a letter from Major Benton Fletcher who had purchased Cedar House some fifteen years previously, alleging 'the town planning scheme subsequently marked out my property for "Industrial Development"!'.

Fortunately the building survived intact for a further twenty years and Hillier's *Old Surrey Water Mills* contains a full description of the buildings as they were in 1951. The author refers to the dangerous bottleneck caused by the larger of the two buildings jutting out into the road and comments that 'it is a matter for marvel that the mill has not been pulled down in the interest of road safety'. (In 1906, the County Surveyor had ordered 'Motor Danger' signals to be fixed at points on the Stoke Road, east and west of the mill). Hillier's words were prophetic and the larger building was demolished in 1953.

The surviving mill is one and a half storeys to the eaves of the steeply pitched, mansard roof. There is no first floor to the mill and the single pair of millstones is mounted on a table-like hurst frame. The two wheels have survived. One is a typical open-cast iron wheel 12ft 6in in diameter and 12ft wide. The other is of similar diameter but only 3ft wide and is made entirely of metal.

Whereas Cobham Mill has only survived in part, the lesser known mill at Downside remains intact, though hidden from public view on the Cobham Park Estate. The buildings here date from the 18th and 19th centuries and show evidence of the many purposes which the mill has served.

Downside Mill belonged to the mediaeval manor of Downe which, in the fourteenth century, was required to make annual payments to Chertsey Abbey of nine gallons of honey for allowing its tenants to grind their own corn here. The Downs estate was connected with a family of that name who had lived here since at least the thirteenth century. In 1565 Thomas a Down of Cobham and Thomas Lyfield of Stoke D'Abernon entered into an agreement. This allowed the former to have access to the mill from the Stoke side of the river to repair and operate the mill, while Lyfield was allowed to take fish in the river twice in each summer, when Down shut up the sluices and floodgates.

In 1720, Lady Lanesborough of Down Place reached agreement with the occupier of the mill to pen the water below it so that the river might flood and thereby irrigate the Down Place meadows. The mill was then described as comprising both paper and corn mills. The Cobham parish registers of 1687 record the baptism of a paper maker's daughter and *Read's Weekly Journal* for 16 June 1733 reported that the paper mill was burnt down, possibly by arson.

John Hillyer, a Cobham churchwarden, occupied Down Mill in 1741 and he was probably the later bookseller of Cobham.

In 1773 the mill was occupied by Messrs Raby and Mereton, iron masters. Raby was there in 1780 and William Hillyer was the freeholder. Raby was an ambitious and fairly distinguished entrepreneur in the iron trade. He later secured interests in several other local water mills, using Downside as his headquarters. Raby converted Downside Mill for the fabrication of iron goods and was active here for about thirty years. There were several mill houses, iron mills, presses, forges and a blacksmith's cottage. Raby left the district for South Wales in about 1810 and set up business in Llanelli.

In 1814 the Vestry minutes recorded 'the Iron Mills being dismantled, Messrs. Jackson & Co should be charged for the House and Garden at the Rate of £35 per year'. By 1825 the premises were used as a flock or rag mill. In 1839 seven men and one woman over the age of 21 years were employed together with eleven boys and youths. There was one wheel producing thirty horse power.

Downside mill was purchased by Charles Combe in 1865 for £3,150 and he installed a nearby generator wheel to produce electricity for Cobham Park. A small water wheel was later installed in the grounds of the house by the Suffolk firm of Whitmore and Binyon to convey water there. The mill at Downside is now used as a builder's yard and some restoration may be carried out in future.

Windmills were also once a common feature of the Surrey landscape. One stood on the edge of the Fairmile Common in the early 19th century, near the present Fairmile Hotel. In 1815 James Thorp occupied it, and in 1851, Thomas Bowel and his assistant.

ABOVE: Cobham Mill, c1890, OPPOSITE ABOVE: c1905, and BELOW: shortly after partial demolition.

ABOVE: An extract from 'The Mill Pond' by Spencer Stanhope — a Pre-Raphaelite view of the Mill. BELOW: Signatures of Thomas Lucy of Cobham Mill and Alexander Raby of Downside Mill from the Cobham Vestry Book — 1772.

ABOVE: The wheel at Downside Mill from Hillier's *Surrey Water Mills*.
BELOW LEFT: Receipt given by Thomas Lucy to Thomas Page in 1784, and
RIGHT: part of the agreement for the sale of Cobham Mill made between
Thomas Page and Thomas Lucy in 1778.

81

The Whitmore & Binyon Water Wheel installed in the grounds of Cobham Park in 1884 to pump water to the house, c1890.

# *Painshill*

Without a doubt, the greatest attraction in eighteenth century Cobham was the landscape park at Painshill created by the Hon Charles Hamilton. Although actually in the adjoining parish of Walton on Thames, Painshill is nearer the centre of Cobham than that of Walton. During the eighteenth and nineteenth centuries, the estate included property in Cobham parish and was, and still is always referred to as 'Painshill, Cobham'.

Hamilton was born in 1704 and was the youngest son of James, 6th Earl of Abercorn. He was educated at Westminster School and Christchurch College, Oxford. He went on the Grand Tour of Europe in 1725 and again in 1732. It is said that in Italy he made friends with many of the leading patrician families there and spent some time collecting antiquities and pictures which he sent home.

On his return to England, Hamilton became one of the Clerks of the Household to Frederick, Prince of Wales, who was then living at Kew. Hamilton looked for an estate nearby and found and purchased the land at Painshill which he seems to have acquired from William Bellamy (c1672-1733), a successful and wealthy barrister who acquired extensive land holdings shortly before his death. Hamilton used this, together with other land acquired by lease and purchase over the following years, to create his masterpiece. Hamilton borrowed heavily from his friend Henry Fox, later Lord Holland.

The land which Hamilton acquired was described by Horace Walpole as 'a cursed hill' and, it is said, was mostly heathland. There were two or three small farms whose histories can be traced back for many centuries and these may have been merged by Bellamy into one holding. Another owner of the land shortly before Hamilton was Gabriel, Marquis De Quesne, a colourful Frenchman of noble ancestry whose grandfather had been one of France's most famous admirals. De Quesne may have carried out a certain amount of parkmaking at Painshill and he may have built the house which became Hamilton's residence.

From the heath and farm land, and whatever improvements had been made by his predecessors, Hamilton created his idea of Paradise. Others such as William Kent were busy as landscape gardeners at this time but, whereas they sought to improve natural landscape by the creation of theatrical set pieces and eye catchers, Hamilton's vision was created from scratch. It was a three dimensional canvas into which the admirer might step and explore.

Just ten years later Hamilton's park had become famous throughout the country and visitors, always welcome, flocked to see it. Small pony-drawn carts were available for hire at the local inns for those who did not care to walk and the park was freely accessible to all who wished to view it. William Bray, the historian of Surrey, was here in 1797 and John Wesley came on at least three occasions and wrote of its beauty in his *Journal*. Horace Walpole, another visitor, wrote that 'All is great and foreign and rude; the walks seem not designed, but cut through the woods of pines; and the style of the whole is so grand, and conducted with so serious an air of wild and uncultivated extent, that when you look down on this seeming forest, you are amazed to find it contains a very few acres'. Walpole's friend, the poet Gray, wrote in 1754 of 'Mr. Hamilton's at Cobham . . . which all the world talks of and I have seen seven years ago.'

Two American presidents, Thomas Jefferson and John Adams visited the park as did John Wilkes, the parliamentary reformer, who wrote of how he 'sauntered through the elysium of Mr. Hamilton's gardens 'til eight in the evening, like the first solitary man through Paradise'.

Having acquired the land, Hamilton set about shifting enormous amounts of soil to create a lake surrounded by steep terrain, some of which was planted to resemble Alpine scenery. The lake was eventually extended to twenty acres but was so designed that it should never all be seen at once, thereby deceiving the visitor into thinking it was even larger. A number of decorative bridges were erected, one of which, the 'Chinese Bridge' has survived. Following the creation of suitable terrain, Hamilton planted trees and shrubs in great numbers, each strategically placed to give specific impressions. Hamilton was a keen arboriculturist and many of the trees were imported from overseas. Some of the earliest rhododendrons to be grown in the country were planted at Painshill. In addition to importing trees, Hamilton also exported a number of specimens as well as seeds. The great cedars of lebanon, now a feature of the park, include one which is thought to be the largest in Europe.

One writer has commented that Painshill was designed as a garden of mood which changed from one part of the park to another. The mood was helped by a series of garden buildings or follies, such as the Temple of Bacchus, the Roman Mausoleum, the Gothick Abbey — built as a ruin — and the attractive Gothick pavilion perched on a hill overlooking the lake.

The centrepiece of the follies was the Grotto, a great cavern constructed in brick and plaster and decorated with crystals and artificial stalactites. The central chamber is now, unfortunately, in a ruinous state, but enough remains of the forty-feet room with its side openings giving views of the lake, to imagine something of its earlier splendour, when the sun, reflected from the surface of the surrounding water, would have sparkled on the crystal ceiling.

In another part of the park was the Hermitage, of rustic appearance with roots and logs. This was the home of the almost legendary hermit employed by Hamilton at a reputedly enormous salary and whose conditions of service included silence at all times. In addition he was to wear 'a camlet robe', use an hour glass for his time piece, never trim his beard or nails, nor stray outside the grounds. The story continues that the unfortunate man was discovered after only three weeks, supping ale in a local public house.

Other follies included an elaborate Turkish Tent, constructed from canvas and brick, a Roman Bath House and a Tower, or Castle, from which three counties could be seen on a clear day, as could Windsor Castle and, sometimes, St Paul's Cathedral in London.

The lake, which was the central feature of the park, is at a level higher than the river Mole which feeds it. Hamilton overcame this by an ingenious horse-drawn engine for raising water, which was illustrated in *The Gentleman's Magazine*. In the 1830s the existing wheel of 36ft diameter was constructed by the engineering firm of Bramah. The water entered the lake through an artificial rockwork cascade. Bramahs are also thought to have been responsible for the former suspension bridge which crossed the Portsmouth Road and linked the house with the farm.

Part of Hamilton's work was of a commercial nature. The vineyard, which occupied a south-facing slope overlooking the lake, produced a sparkling white wine which was sufficiently good to deceive the French ambassador into believing it to be champagne. The wine was sold in the local inns at 7s 6d a bottle, a considerable sum in those days. William Cobbett recorded having visited the vineyard when he was a child. Remains of a brick or tileworks have recently been uncovered.

In addition to the lake and its immediate landscaped area, Hamilton created contrasting 'open views' across the verdant pasture land near the present house.

Hamilton's house, of which only a fragment now remains, stood near the Portsmouth Road on the brow of the hill, and was probably an enlargement of the house constructed by De Quesne.

The present house was built by Benjamin Bond Hopkins, who purchased the estate in 1773, when Hamilton retired to Bath to continue his landscaping activities from a house in the Royal Crescent. Bond Hopkins' architect was Richard Jupp. The house is of a simple but elegant design and was planned as a five-bayed, two-storeyed villa with a large porch of four composite columns to the east and a bow to the west. Single storeyed, colonnaded wings originally extended either side to hexagonal pavilions, which have long since disappeared.

Architect Decimus Burton made a number of alterations and additions to the house in the first half of the nineteenth century, and it was nearly completely rebuilt by Richard Norman Shaw in the 1880s. Shaw had prepared plans for a large pseudo-Tudor House, in true Victorian baronial style but fortunately, he was only permitted to execute a service wing on one side. The removal of the great portico may have been his doing. It was replaced by a simple wooden verandah which, in turn, was replaced by the present portico from the Temple of Bacchus. A number of designs for the ceiling of that building were made by the noted architect Robert Adam and it may be that he was responsible for the whole building and, possibly, other garden buildings.

The house contains some fine interior decoration, especially in the entrance hall, inner hall and saloon, which looks across the river Mole to Cobham.

Both house and park passed through a succession of owners during the nineteenth century, including the Earl of Carhampton, who moved here from Cobham Park, W.H. Cooper, High Sherriff of Surrey, and C.J. Leaf, a city merchant and philanthropist whose friend, the poet Matthew Arnold came to live at Pains Hill Cottage and was allowed to use the park as if it were his own. The estate eventually passed into the ownership of the Combe family of Cobham Park and remained their property for many years. There are still some of Cobham's older residents who can recall visits here for Sunday School treats and Empire Day Sports, when Mrs Combe was in residence.

During the last world war, the estate was requisitioned by the Army and, unfortunately, considerable damage was done in the park, particularly to the Grotto. After the war, the estate was sold to Baroness De Veauce, who later split it up and sold it off in lots.

For many years the park lay forgotten to all but a few. One garden historian who recognised its importance and who came here during those forgotten years wrote of the 'power and wealth of Nature' at Painshill, 'the mighty trees — the holly, the chestnuts, the cedars of lebanon and the solitary pines — which strike the dominant chord in this magnificent park symphony, and of the shimmering surfaces of water from which the light vibrates between the trees, banishing all gloom and keeping alive that vision of Elysium that was once realised here'.

In recent years a small group of Friends of Painshill persuaded the local authority to acquire the major part of the park and the Painshill Trust has now been set up, not only to own and administer the park, but also to restore it all to Hamilton's original concept, and thereby preserve a unique facet of a major English contribution to the world of visual arts.

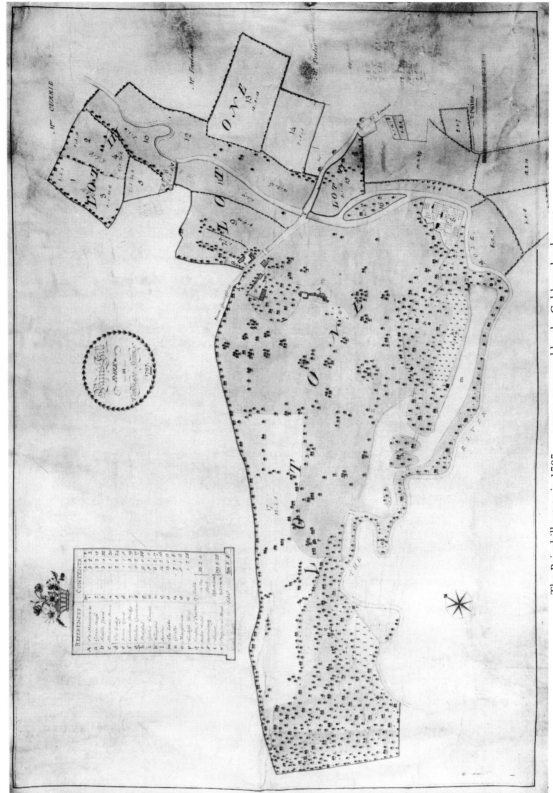

The Painshill estate in 1797 — a map prepared by the Cobham land agent and surveyor Thomas Crawter.

The Hon Charles Hamilton (1704-1786); painted in Rome in 1732 by
Antonio David.

ABOVE: Painshill House and Cobham Bridge from an engraving of 1787;
Charles Hamilton's house can just be seen by the bridge over the
Portsmouth Road, and BELOW: 'A Scene in the Gardens of Painshill' — a
none too accurate view.

# Particulars.

THE CELEBRATED AND MUCH ADMIRED DOMAIN OF

# PAINS HILL,

Is situated in the Parishes of COBHAM and WALTON, in the County of SURREY, immediately adjoining the former Village, and within 18 miles of London, in a highly select and desirable neighbourhood. It is divided into two unequal portions by the high Turnpike Road to Portsmouth, over which (connecting the two) is a Wooden Bridge.

In the southern and larger portion of the Estate is

# THE MANSION,

An elegant structure, placed on a delightful Terrace, commanding beautiful views, and from whence is a Lawn gradually sloping to the River Mole, which flows through the Grounds. The principal Front is represented in the annexed view, and has its centre decorated with Four lofty Columns, with a Flight of Steps at their base, finished on each side by Stone Blockings, surmounted by Sphynxes. It possesses every requisite accommodation for a numerous Establishment, and contains

### On the Upper Floor,

SIX VERY GOOD ATTICS.

### On the First Floor,

*FIVE BEST BED ROOMS and FIVE DRESSING ROOMS.*

### A Morning Room or Boudoir.

A FRENCH BED ROOM; a Water Closet, and a Store Closet on the Landing.

### On the Principal Floor,

## AN ELEGANT ENTRANCE HALL,

Of oval shape, with niches for Figures or Lamps, 29 feet 3 by 18 feet 9, with folding doors opening to the Back Front, from whence is a double Flight of Steps leading to the Coach Sweep approach.

THE ENTRANCE HALL COMMUNICATES WITH

### An Inner Hall,

Containing a STORE CLOSET and STRONG ROOM; and an ELEGANT STONE STAIR-CASE, lighted from the top, conducts to the Gallery of the First Floor.

### A LIBRARY, or MORNING ROOM.

A GENTLEMAN'S DRESSING ROOM; a Back Stair-case, communicating with two Water Closets; and

### A BATH ROOM.

From the Inner Hall, and occupying the centre of the Principal Front, is

## THE SALOON,

29 feet 6 long, 19 feet 6 wide, and 15 feet high, with a pair of French Sash Windows opening to the Flight of Steps leading to the Terrace.

89

# THE GROUNDS

Surrounding the Mansion, combine all the attractions that a happily diversified and highly favoured spot, sided by consummate skill, can present. They have been often described, and have been cited* as the most beautiful and interesting specimen of Landscape Gardening on a large scale, perhaps, in Europe. Their formation was the triumph of the genius and taste, in this delightful art, of The Honorable CHARLES HAMILTON, and at an enormous expence. In attempting an outline of some of their principal beauties, much must inevitably be omitted.—Beginning at the Mansion, the length and space of the Terrace must be noticed, with its wide spreading Cedars and branching Oaks, and the views enjoyed from it of the adjacent country.—More to the Southward is a Hill, whose summit has been levelled and planted, and where the Cork Tree and other natives of more sultry climes, flourish near the Northern Fir and Pine. At the ridge of this Hill is

## A GOTHIC TEMPLE,

Commanding a view of

## THE SPACIOUS LAKE,

With its ISLANDS and elegant CONNECTING BRIDGE. On the border of the Lake is

## The Magnificent Grotto,

Supposed to be the finest in England : the whole of its interior is encrusted with the Derbyshire Stalactyte, while masses of artificial Rock Work are disposed near the entrance, and in different parts, with great effect, and a CASCADE falling within a Cavern in the inmost recesses of the Grotto, escapes by devious channels into the Lake.

AT A SHORT DISTANCE FROM THE ABOVE IS

## AN ANCIENT MAUSOLEUM,

Containing some antique Marble Sarcophagi and Cineraria.

On an eminence beyond the Lake is

## An ERECTION, in the form of a TURKISH TENT,

Favorably placed for the view of the water and home scenery ; and further beyond is the

### BEAUTIFUL

## DORIC TEMPLE,

Copied from the *Maison Carré* at Nismes, and called the TEMPLE OF BACCHUS ; the Entrance Front having a Portico with a fine and appropriate alto-relievo in the pediment.

Still further, and near the extremity of the Grounds, in the midst of a Forest of majestic Pine and Fir Trees, stands

## A TOWER

Of great height, built in imitation of a Watch Tower of the middle ages ; from the top of which most extensive prospects of the surrounding country may be obtained.

## THE MACHINERY

For filling the Lake, and supplying the House with Water, deserves to be mentioned :—it consists of an under-shot Wheel of great diameter, with levers, &c.; and a Cistern on high land, from whence is a lead pipe to the Mansion.

IN ADDITION TO THE ABOVE, THERE ARE

A COLD BATH, a HERMITAGE, a FISHING HOUSE, LABOURERS' COTTAGES, **Summer House, &c.**

And GROTPES and VASES decorate various parts of the Grounds.

* "Horace Walpole on Landscape Gardening."
"Illustrations of Surrey," &c. &c.

---

ON THE RIGHT OF THE SALOON ARE

## Two very elegant Drawing Rooms,

Measuring together 55 feet long and 18 feet wide ; the walls panelled and stuccoed in light blue and gilt, with decorated ceilings painted in medallions ; the doors grained to represent satin-wood and air-wood.

ON THE LEFT OF THE SALOON IS

## A DINING PARLOR,

27 feet by 18 ; one end having Two scagliola Pillars with bronzed capitals ; the sides of the Room with panels, containing beautiful Paintings of Landscapes and Figures ; and over the doors *bas-relief*, representing the Fine Arts.

## A CORRIDOR,

With groined ceiling, (having a communication also with the Basement) leads from the smaller Drawing Room to the

## GOTHIC CHAPEL,

Which is 33 feet long and 24 feet 6 wide, and is fitted up with great taste ; the windows filled with stained glass ; the walls panelled all round, 4 feet 5 from the Floor, with Oak ; one end raised, elliptically shaped, and fitted up with carved Oak Stalls ; on one side is a Recess, 8 feet 9 by 5 feet 3, with folding glazed doors, opening into a FLOWER GARDEN, in which is an AVIARY, a POND for Gold and Silver Fish, and communication with the Terrace.

### The Basement

CONTAINS

A Butler's Pantry, and a Strong Closet from ditto with iron door.
A Servant's Hall, with entrance from the back front.
A Larder.
Man Servant's Room.
A Steward's Room.
Ale Cellar, and Wine Cellars.
Two Store Closets.
Housekeeper's Room, and Housekeeper's Store Room.
A Passage leading to a capital KITCHEN, 27 feet by 23 feet 6, with Scullery adjoining.

In a Court Yard connected with the Offices, and enclosed by Gates, are

Game Larders ; Charcoal, Coal, Wood and Sand Houses ; Wash-house, Laundry, Mangle Rooms, Three Bed Room, Bake-house, and

## A TASTEFUL DAIRY,

With Gothic Windows and Stone Floor.

*Detached are* COACH-HOUSES *and* STABLING, *with Lofts and Mens' Rooms over ;* Granary, Brew-house, &c.

NEAR THE MANSION IS A RANGE OF

## TWO VERY SPACIOUS GREEN-HOUSES,

Filled with rare Exotics ; and

## An Orangery.

THERE ARE

## THREE KITCHEN GARDENS,

At a short distance from the Mansion, walled all round, and are reckoned some of the most productive in Surrey ; with extensive ranges of

**Hot Houses, Grapery and Peach Houses, Gardeners' Cottages, Tool Houses, Sheds, &c.**

---

ABOVE & OVER: The Painshill Sale Catalogue of 1831. OPPOSITE ABOVE: 'A View From The West Side Of The Island In The Garden Of The Hon. Charles Hamilton Esq. At Painshill Near Cobham In Surrey'; an engraving by W. Woolett from the mid-eighteenth century. The Turkish Tent, Temple of Bacchus and Castle can just be seen. BELOW: View From The Temple Of Bacchus by the Swedish artist Elias Martin.

91

ABOVE LEFT: Painshill House and Cobham Bridge from an engraving of 1820. CENTRE: The Gothic Pavilion in the early nineteenth century, BELOW & RIGHT: and in 1966.

ABOVE LEFT: The Bramah Water Wheel for raising water from the river to feed the lake. RIGHT: The Gothic Ruin and BELOW LEFT: the Roman Mausoleum (1966), and RIGHT: the Castle (1966) before damage by fire and vandalism.

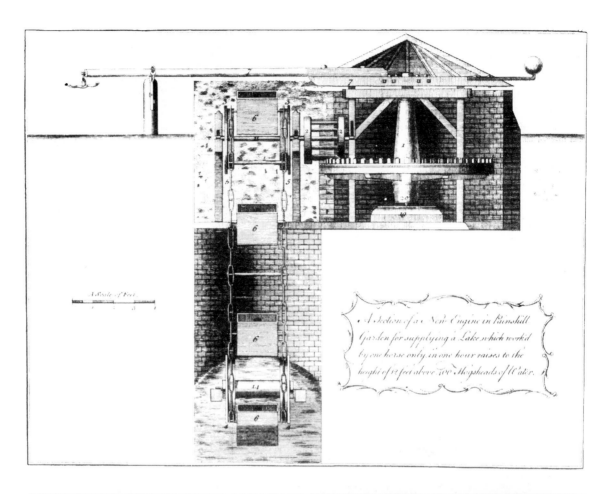

A Scale of Feet.

A Section of a New Engine in Painshill Garden for supplying a Lake which work'd by one horse only, in one hour raises to the height of 12 feet above 700 Hogsheads of Water.

ABOVE: An ingenious machine for raising water at Painshill, from an engraving in the *Gentleman's Magazine,* 1771, and LEFT: the Grotto in 1966, with RIGHT: one of the giant Cedars nearby.

ABOVE: The Bramah Suspension Bridge that formerly linked Painshill House and Farm over the Portsmouth Road, and BELOW: R. Norman Shaw's unexecuted design for a new house at Painshill.

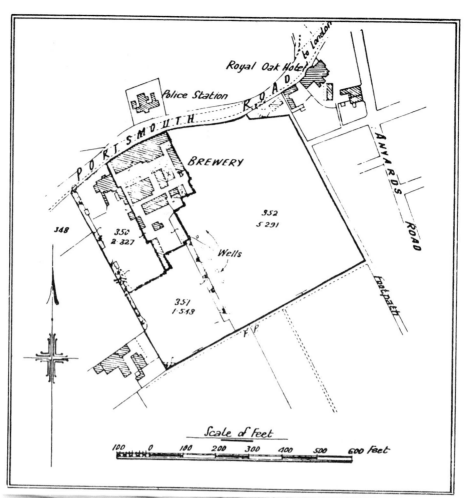

ABOVE: Cobham Brewery — a plan from 1924, and BELOW: bottle
washers at the Brewery.

96

# In Their Own Time

Long working hours and agricultural labour left little time for all but the more wealthy of our ancestors to engage in leisurely pursuits. Such holidays as existed were either those granted by the lords of the manors or the holy days of the church. The seasonal fairs which gave occasion for some relaxation from work usually had some religious significance.

The physiography of Cobham became the source for what local recreation there was while other entertainments were introduced by custom or need. The proximity of the river Mole meant that fishing was more than a pastime, and the surrounding countryside gave opportunity for hunting and equestrian sports.

Until the late nineteenth century, the only regular excitement for ordinary people was provided by the local ale house. In 1605 Cobham had '2 inns and 5 alehouses, 3 too many'. The pubs of Cobham, which numbered about fifteen by the 1850s, gave the place a certain notoriety for lack of abstinence. 'Drenched in drink and wickedness' was how one visiting clergyman described Cobham in 1861. The fact that one of Cobham's major sources of employment at this time was a brewery did nothing to help allay that reputation.

For many centuries, brewing was a home industry. There were no breweries as we know them today and the beer available in the alehouses would have been brewed on the premises. It appears that the brewery which flourished in Cobham for at least 120 years grew out of the premises of John Louis Mackay, described in 1803 as 'All that Cottage or Tenement . . . known by the name of Homes Place with the Malthouse Brewhouse Yard and Garden therunto belonging'. In 1806 Mackay sold the building to Joseph Stedman of Cedar House and it was he who established the business on a firm footing. On Stedman's death, the brewery passed to his daughter and then to her son, Richard Wallis Ashby and became known as 'Ashby's Cobham Brewery'. Ashby was much respected in Cobham and was both 'a good churchman and a good sportsman' who did 'excellent work in the schools' and who helped to bring the gas supply to the village.

Most of the pubs in Cobham were, at some time, either owned or controlled by Ashby, the only exceptions being the Tartar and the White Lion. Many of those pubs have long since disappeared and are remembered in name only. One was the Crown which stood in the High Street on the site of Threshold Records and which, in 1795, was described as 'all that customary messuage or tenement called The Crown Inn . . . with the stableyard privy and garden a Butchers Shop adjoining the said messuage the sign and the sign post'. Opposite, on the corner of Church Street and High Street, stood the Fox and Hounds, at one time managed by Henry Glanville, son of John Glanville who kept the Crown. The Fox was probably the successor to an older ale house called the White Hart which, in 1756, stood on the opposite corner of Church Street.

Other former pubs were the Swan which stood on the Portsmouth Road, near the White Lion, and which was pulled down in the early eighteenth century; the Waggon and Horses on the Downside Road, which later became part of Cobham Stud; the Royal Oak, near the corner of Anyards Road and Portsmouth Road, which was managed by Sutton Porter in 1753; and the King's Arms, later the Cobham Motor Works, which stood on the site of the Murco Service Station near Cobham Bridge. In 1838, the King's Arms United Brothers Benefit Society met here.

97

The Antelope on the Portsmouth Road is the successor to the George, destroyed by fire in the middle of the last century, and the Harrow at Downside was demolished some years ago. The Old Bear on River Hill, another Cobham Brewery pub, is thought to date from the late 15th century and was perhaps originally three cottages. In 1719, the Bear was occupied by John Jacob and, in 1721, a boy baptised at Cobham was named Richard Bear, born at the Bear, son of a stroller or actor. In 1781, the Manorial Court of Cobham dined at the Bear, paying Sarah Downton £5 15s 6d, nearly half of which was for wine and beer.

In 1888 the Cobham Brewery also owned the Little White Lion, the Running Mare and the Plough at Stoke D'Abernon. In 1913 the Brewery became Cobham United Breweries Ltd and eventually closed down in 1922. The premises were purchased by Watney Combe Reid & Co. who used them as an off licence and store. The last of the brewery buildings was demolished in 1970. Cobham had two other indirect connections with the brewing industry through Joseph Moss, a partner in Charrington's Brewery, who lived in Cedar House in 1765, and Harvey Combe of Cobham Park, whose London Brewery became part of Watney Combe Reid & Co.

For those who sought more health-giving refreshment, Cobham could offer mineral water from a number of natural springs in the area. One was at Goose Green, Downside which had been discovered about 1670. John Aubrey wrote 'At Cobham is a medicated Spring of the nature of Epsham which was discovered about three years since by a country-man useing it in his food: as also giving it to his pigges which he putt to fatting: I am told at the bottome of this Well are Stones like Bristow-diamonds'. Bristol Diamonds are crystals of colourless quartz and were worn by ladies of rank. In 1736 the water was considered superior to that at Epsom but by 1823 it had gone out of fashion.

Another spa is at Spa Bottom on the Fairmile. In 1736 it was said that 'There is a well called Fairmile Water of the Tunbridge kind, but far exceeding those in virtue'. The Universal British Directory of 1793 stated 'In this parish are two medicinal springs, Cobham-Wells and the Spa, which were formerly much resorted to; but have been some time in disrepute on account of Jessop's Well, which is in the vicinity'.

Jessop's Well was on Stoke Common outside Cobham parish, and its little brick building still stands in Prince's Coverts, Oxshott. In the eighteenth century the water was sold at Owen's Mineral Water Warehouse at Temple Bar in Fleet Street. A man who merely stood bare-legged in the well to clean it, was purged severely for a week, and Dr Adee of Guildford said that the water would act smartly, and that a cautious use of it had happy consequences.

One of the ancient privileges of the Manor of Cobham was that of holding a fair on the feast of St Andrew, patron saint of the parish church. The fair was for cows, steers, horses, sheep, and pigs and was held until about 1859 in a field at Street Cobham, on the site now occupied by the house called Faircroft. In 1796 a meadow near Downside Bridge was known as Fair Meadow and was possible the site of an earlier fair. King Stephen had granted the Abbot of Chertsey the right to hold a Tuesday Market in Cobham and, in the late eighteenth century, a fair for 'toys and pleasures' was held on March 17 in each year.

For many years the Tilt Green was used for May Day celebrations and a maypole was erected there during the last century. It seems that the very success of the fairs proved their downfall. Gypsies and fair people descended on the Green with 'vans of all sorts and kinds with shows, these large steam merry-go-rounds, etc . . . They brought about 70 horses; which were a great annoyance to those living nearby, besides about a dozen wretched donkeys, quite new last year'. Sufficient local opposition gathered for official posters to be printed saying that no more fairs were to be held on the common, and the last was held in 1902.

Fishing was, of course, more than a leisure pursuit and there were important manorial fishing rights in the river Mole. A fishery at Cobham Bridge was granted by Charles II to Thomas Wyndham, whose wife Elizabeth had assisted the King's escape after the battle of Worcester.

Bream and tench were noted here in 1744 and, in the early nineteenth century, an eel weir was erected across the Mole by the lord of the manor. In 1840 it was stated that 'there is some good angling for pike and perch between Pains Hill and Esher Place; occasionally a few trout may be taken with the fly, but they are gradually disappearing, the natural result of the all destroying pike'. The author of *Rambles By Rivers* (1844) wrote that Cobham 'must be very refreshing in its quietness to the many anglers who escape to it from the noise of London'. Fishing remains a popular local pastime and there are thriving angling clubs in the district.

In the reign of Henry I, Cobham, like most of Surrey, was in Windsor Forest and the King found it profitable to grant the privilege of destroying animals harmful to the beasts of the Royal hunt. After 1190, Windsor Forest came no nearer to Cobham than Byfleet Bridge. Part of Cobham was enclosed in the chase of Hampton Court in about 1540. The return of parts of Cobham to forest law caused great hardship to many villagers for only the King and his courtiers were allowed to hunt here.

Hunting of both stag and fox remained a popular pursuit for centuries. The French royal family, exiled at nearby Claremont, would hunt carted deer in the neighbourhood. The local hunt was the Surrey Union, which moved its kennels to Cobham Court in 1902. Thomas Henry Bennett of Cobham Court served as Master of Fox Hounds for many years.

Fox hunting petered out after the First World War. Electrification of the local railway line brought the final blow when hounds were injured crossing the line. The last stag to be hunted in Cobham was so tame that it had to be fed with the horses. On its last day out, it jumped into the flooded Mole near the Mill, where it was killed by the pursuing hounds. The Crowhurst Otter Hunt also met frequently at Cobham, which was said to be one of their best meets.

Surprising though it may seem now, horse racing was once a local entertainment, the sport taking place on the Tilt in the eighteenth century. Cheyney's Calender refers to two races run on Cobham Tilt in 1734 for prizes of 15 and 20 guineas. In the next year there was a three day meet and in 1737 Mr Harpur's Creeping Kate was 'thrown by a man in the way'. The Running Mare took its name from this time and was first known as the Running Horse. By 1784 the pub had assumed its present name — a name reputed to be unique in England.

Horse racing had died out on the Tilt by 1780 but Cobham was again linked with the turf in the following century, with the establishment of the Cobham Stud Company at Cobham Park. The fortunes of the Stud were based on a famous stallion, Blair Athol, the 'Blaze-faced King of Cobham' which was purchased by the company for £13,000. In the course of his life this horse produced no less than 60 yearlings and in the 1896 Derby, five of the runners were his progeny.

In 1896 the annual sale of yearlings meant 'a special train down from town for the occasion, and this was fairly well filled; but apparently most of the travellers went in for the inspection and for the free luncheon rather than for the business in as much as there were very few purchasers'. According to the autobiography of William Allison, the manager of the Stud, this particular sale attracted the Prince of Wales, later Edward VII, accompanied by Lillie Langtry. The Prince is also reported to have been a visitor to Stoke Lodge for the polo matches played nearby.

Cricket was another popular use for the Tilt Green and Alexander Raby, the Downside iron master, recorded in a letter of 1822 that 'I am as well as ever tho I cannot run as fast or jump as high as when Ld. Tankerville, Sr. Francis Vincent, his brother and we used to play at cricket upon the Tilt 50 years ago'. The Tilt's great cricketing days were in the closing years of the last century when a local man, and Surrey player Fred Stedman would often bring the County down to play the home team. Local enthusiasm for the Tilt Club was demonstrated by the offer of Roland Weller, proprietor of the adjacent carriage works, to give £5 and a bottle of whisky to the first player to hit a boundary through his bedroom window.

The Cobham United Cricket Club was formed in the 1880s and had its first ground at Pyports Field and then on the White Lion Meadow. In 1887 it was decided to build a pavilion 'at a not greater cost than £15 and to engage a man for three months to look after the grounds etc at 20/–per week'. The Tilt Club eventually petered out due largely to increasing traffic on the Stoke Road and the likelihood of boundary accidents.

Football has long been another popular local sport, and local teams such as Cobham Hawks were playing regular matches in the late nineteenth century. In 1886 a Football Club was formed in connection with the local Coffee Tavern, and the Vicar offered to supply the proposed club with its first football. The present Cobham Football Club has its grounds on the Leg Of Mutton Field. A local swimming club existed for some years, making use of the river Mole. Changing rooms were provided on the banks of the river near the Tilt.

Most of Cobham's recreational facilities have now been transferred to the Recreation Ground of Anyards Road, laid out on fields which formerly belonged to the Cobham Brewery. There are tennis courts and a bowling green as well as football pitches and a children's playing area. The nearest indoor sports complex is at Leatherhead, although Walton has an indoor swimming pool.

Until the last century, Cobham lacked any proper indoor meeting room or club facilities. Public meetings were generally held at the White Lion and other pubs provided rooms for hire. A parish room became available at the Tilt when the former school room closed down, and the opening of the new schools in Cedar Road provided a hall suitable for concerts and small gatherings. In 1877 C.J. Leaf of Painshill, a city merchant and philanthropist, provided Street Cobham with a Temperance Hall which later became the Cobham Working Men's Club. The old iron building was demolished in 1981 and a new village club now stands on the site.

The present Village Hall was opened in 1888 on a site given by T.H. Bennett of Cobham Court. Charles Combe gave £500 towards the new building and other subscribers included W.S. Deacon of Pointers, Vernon Lushington of Pyports, R.W. Ashby of Cobham Brewery and Matthew Arnold. The hall was speedily built by Mr Newland, the local builder, who also built the Downside Working Mens Club, and the opening concert was supervised by Howard Paul, a noted American actor and playwright who had achieved popularity in English music halls.

The new hall was immediately set to use with a number of concerts, some of which were arranged by the talented Lushington sisters, and in which they invited family friends to take part. Guy Du Maurier, uncle of the novelist Daphne Du Maurier was one who trod the boards at Cobham Village Hall and it is possible that the young Ralph Vaughan Williams, a cousin by marriage, may have performed there. In 1889 the newly formed Cobham Brass Band 'discoursed sweet music from the vestibule' of the hall. The band had originally been installed in the gallery but 'their instruments having been chosen for their carrying effect in the open air, proved rather overpowering to sensitive ears'.

The hall was put to many uses, including religious and political meetings, hunt balls and, in 1894, the inaugural meeting of the Parish Council. Edison's phonograph and 'the new X rays' were demonstrated to the local people in 1890 and 1896 respectively. In August 1914, the hall 'was packed with Cobham men eager to hear of their country's need and to declare their willingness to render personal service in whatever way their age and opportunities made possible'.

In the years following the First War, the hall served as a library, dentist's surgery, clinic and cinema (Cobham's own cinema, the Savoy, on the Portsmouth Road, closed in 1965).

In 1938, the *Daily Mirror* carried the headline: 'Dance Morals Trial Held Up By Roars Of Village'. Councillor Thomas Daly, a trustee of the hall had, according to *John Bull* magazine, 'claimed that "the orgies which take place after these hectic hops" rival those of Sodom and Gomorrah, the "disgusting scenes" presented included first aids to nausea as "girls and boys cuddling and kissing in dark corner".' A public enquiry was held at the village hall and the press had a field day with headlines such as 'Cobham Village Hall "Orgies" Inquiry'. During the course of the enquiry Daly was accused of being a 'trouble making, scandal mongering, publicity loving, dishonest old man'. The outcome of the proceedings was that Daly's statement 'though he eventually limited his complaint to two occasions, seems to have been made very wildly and without taking reasonable steps to ascertain the facts'. The *Daily Mail* announced 'Surrey's Cobham is no Gomorrah. The Village has been vindicated'.

The excitement soon died down and the episode was overshadowed by the Second World War, when the hall was used as a gas mask distribution depot, a First Aid Post, an ARP centre and a British Restaurant.

In recent years the hall has been extensively modernised but it now seems likely that a new one will be built, on a site next to Cobham Day Centre, and the old hall demolished, thus ending an era in local entertainment.

TO BREWERS, MANUFACTURERS, AND OTHERS.
HIGHLY IMPORTANT FREEHOLD PROPERTY.
## THE COBHAM BREWERY,
## COBHAM, SURREY.

Having a frontage of 700ft. to the main London and Portsmouth road ; London 17 miles, Esher four miles, and Guildford nine miles.

The Brewery Premises are substantially erected of brick, and consist of several blocks of buildings of one, two, and three storeys, with a total floor space of 3,084 SQ. YDS.

In addition there is a DETACHED PRIVATE RESI-DENCE (three reception, seven bed rooms ; stable, garage). BRICK and TILED BUNGALOW, and VALUABLE BUILDING LAND.

The whole having an area of about 9½ ACRES, which will be offered to Public AUCTION, unless previously sold by Private Treaty, at the London Auction Mart, 155, Queen Victoria-street, E.C.4, on April 10th, 1923, at 2.30 o'clock.—Further particulars of Messrs.

## HEATH & SALTER,
AUCTIONEERS, 15, FARNHAM-ROAD, GUILDFORD.

LEFT: A cutting from *The Times* of 27 March 1923; RIGHT: Woodham Lodge on the Portsmouth Road, the last of the Brewery buildings, demolished in 1970, and BELOW: the former Royal Oak from a painting by William Freeman dated May 1890.

ABOVE: The Royal Oak, c1905, on the Portsmouth Road next to the Brewery, demolished in 1974; CENTRE: the old Fox and Hounds on the corner of Church Street and High Street, rebuilt in the early years of this century and demolished in the 1960s, and BELOW: the Plough at Stoke D'Abernon, c1905.

ABOVE: The Crown, a Cobham Brewery pub, 1904. The building adjoining the Crown, which still stands, was then the Cobham Coffee House and Reading Room, and BELOW: the Little White Lion, c1905.

# The Cobham Amateur Dramatic Club.

Wednesday, May 3rd,
——1905.——

Kindly assisted by the
——Oxshott Club.——

## "AN OLD MASTER."

### Characters:

| | |
|---|---|
| Sir Rupert Vanstone ... | Mr. E. MONIER-WILLIAMS |
| Matthew Penrose ... ... ... | Mr. S. GORDON-CLARK |
| Simpkin (Valet) ... ... ... ... | Mr. C. TROLLOPE |
| Miss Penelope Gamble (Matthew's Sister-in-law) | Miss HELME |
| Sophie Penrose ... ... ... | Miss MURIEL KESWICK |

Scene: Exterior of Matthew's Cottage.

*Time: An August Afternoon.*

## "ICI ON PARLE FRANCAIS."

### Characters:

| | |
|---|---|
| Mr. Spriggins ... ... ... ... | Mr. H. GORING |
| Mrs. Spriggins (his Wife) ... ... | Miss VERREY |
| Angelina (their Daughter) ... ... | Miss MORRISH |
| Anna Maria (Maid of All Work) ... | Miss LAMBERT |
| Major Regulus Rattan (of the Cape Coast Slashers) ... ... | Mr. W. ELLIS |
| Mrs. Rattan (his Wife) ... ... ... | Miss DURRAD |
| Victor Dubois (a Frenchman) ... ... | Mr. R. MORRISH |

Scene: A room in Mr. Spriggins' house
at Dipwell.

K.D.S. LTD. 22904.

ABOVE: Cobham Amateur Dramatic Club Programme from 1905, and
BELOW: Cobham Village Hall, c1910.

## LIST OF MEMBERS.

Abernethy, Miss
Agar, C. T., Esq.
Agar, Mrs.
Bailey, W., Esq.
Bailey, Miss
Bennett, Mrs.
Bishop, W., Esq.
Bishop, Mrs.
Bishop, Miss L.
Bishop, Miss K.
Blackburne, Rev. A. S. P.
Blake, R., Esq.
Blake, Mrs.
Bowen-Buscarlet, Lt.-Col.
Bowen-Buscarlet, Mrs.
Boyd, Miss M.
Bristowe, B. A., Esq.
Bristowe, Mrs.
Bristowe, Miss E.
Brookes, Rev. G. Remfrey
Brookes, Mrs. G. Remfrey
Brookes, Miss G. Remfrey
Brookes, L. Remfrey, Esq.
Cartwright, Miss
Cawston, E., Esq.
Cawston, Mrs.
Cayley, Lady
Chamberlain, Mrs.
Chamberlain, Miss
Clark, Gordon, Col.
Clark, Gordon, Mrs.
Child, S., Esq.
Child, Miss
Collins, Lady
Collinson, Mrs.
Combe, Charles, Esq.
Combe, Mrs. Charles
Combe, C. H., Esq.
Combe, Miss D.
Courtenay, W. Esq.
Courtenay, Miss
Cripps, F. E., Esq.
Cripps, Mrs.
Davies, W. H., Esq.
Davies, Mrs.
Dowson, C., Esq.
Dowson, Mrs.
Dowson, N. Esq.
Dowson, Mrs. N.
Dunning, Sir L.

Dunning, Lady
Gaskell, Dr. H. S.
Grane, Mrs.
Gunnell, D., Esq.
Gunnell, Mrs.
Gwynne, Commander
Gwynne, Mrs.
Hale, Mrs.
Hale, Miss R.
Hale, Miss M.
Hale, Miss
Harrison, L., Esq.
Harrison, Mrs.
Hasloch, G., Esq.
Hasloch, Mrs.
Hasloch, Miss
Hasloch, Miss E.
Harris, S., Esq.
Harris, Mrs.
Heath, W., Esq.
Heath, Mrs.
Helby, J. T., Esq.
Helby, Miss Edith
Helby, Miss W.
Howard, Mrs.
Husband, Miss
Hobson, Mrs.
Hudson, E., Esq.
Hudson, Mrs.
Hervey, Commander
Hervey, Mrs.
Ionides, G., Esq.
Ionides, Mrs. G.
Kitching, Dr. J. L. W.
Kitching, Mrs.
Kitching, Miss B.
Jupp, C. S., Esq.
Lafone, H. C., Esq.
Lafone, Mrs.
Leuchars, W. W., Esq.
Leuchars, Mrs.
Letchworth, O. P., Esq.
Letchworth, Mrs.
Machin, P., Esq.
Machin, Mrs.
Machin, Miss M.
Machin, Miss E.
Mason, A. B., Esq.
Mason, Mrs.
Martin, L., Esq.

Martin, Mrs.
Milward, H., Esq.
Milward, Mrs.
Mercer, J. B., Esq.
Mercer, Mrs.
Mercer, J. L., Esq.
Mercer, Mrs.
Morrish, R. S., Esq.
Mount, Mrs.
Mount, Miss
Nilson F., Esq.
Nilson, Mrs.
Price, H. W., Esq.
Raworth, A., Esq.
Raworth, Mrs.
Robinson, Mrs.
Robinson, Miss
Savory, Mrs.
Samuelson, Sir H. B., Bt.
Samuelson, Lady
Seth-Smith, A., Esq.
Seth-Smith, Mrs.
Seth-Smith, Miss
Seth-Smith, E., Esq.
Shaw, J. H., Esq.
Shaw, Mrs.
Shelford, F., Esq.
Shelford, Mrs.
Smith, F. Clyde, Esq.
Smith, F. Clyde, Mrs.
Steriker, — Esq.
Steriker, Mrs.
Thompson, W. Graham, Esq.
Thompson, Mrs. Graham
Trengrouse, A. P., Esq.
Trengrouse, Mrs.
Thomas, Miss
Thomas, Miss E.
Trollope, Col. G. H.
Trollope, Mrs.
Verrey, Mrs.
Von der Heyde, Miss
Warren, Miss
Walmesley Cotham, Esq.
Walmesley Cotham, Mrs.
Wightwick, E. A., Esq.
Wightwick, Mrs.
Wilson, Mrs. J.
Wigram, R., Esq.
Wigram, Mrs.

## RULES

1. The Club shall be styled **The Cobham Amateur Dramatic Club**, and shall consist of amateurs only.

2. Annual Subscription (entitling Members to free admission to each entertainment), 5s.

3. Each Member is entitled at each entertainment to a reserved seat transferable to a member of the family only. Other seats, according to available space, will be offered for sale. Members are entitled to purchase tickets for any of their family—or for friends staying in the house or friends non-resident in Cobham, before seats are available for the general public.

4. The general management of the Club shall be vested in a Committee consisting of the President, Vice-President, Hon. Secretary and Treasurer, and not less than six other members of the Club, each of whom shall retire annually, but be eligible for re-election at the Annual General Meeting.

5. The Committee shall appoint a Cast Committee of three before each performance, for the purpose of choosing and casting plays, and arranging for their production. The Cast Committee to include on all occasions one Member of the Committee.

6. The Annual General Meeting, ten days' notice of which shall be given, shall be held as soon as possible after the last performance of each season, and the Report and Balance Sheet shall then be submitted to the Club.

7. Candidates shall be proposed and seconded by two Members of the Club, and their elections shall be vested in the Committee, and shall take effect if a majority of the Committee present are in favour thereof.

8. The Club Season shall be from October to April.

9. All Subscriptions to the Club are due on 1st October in each year, and any Member intending to resign shall inform the Secretary in writing before the 30th September.

10. The Committee shall have power to elect Honorary Acting Members at their discretion, and to fill up any vacancy on the Committee.

11. No rule shall be altered except at the Annual General Meeting or at a Special General Meeting of the Club, ten days' notice of which must be given to Members and which must be called on requisition to the Hon. Secretary either by three members of the Committee or by nine members of the Club.

ABOVE: Cobham Amateur Dramatic club — 1919, and BELOW: a hunt meet at Woodlands Park in the 1930s.

# Daily Mirror

No. 10733    Registered at the G.P.O. as a Newspaper.    ONE PENNY

# DANCE MORALS TRIAL
## HELD UP BY ROARS OF VILLAGE

### The Purity Battle of Cobham

Mr. Thomas Richard Daly, the jobbing gardener whose purity campaign case will be presented at to-night's inquiry by the Charity Commissioners in the village hall at Cobham, Surrey.

**R**OARS of laughter, cheers and shouts interrupted last night the Cobham (Surrey) inquiry into dance hall manners, an unofficial court of morals unseen in England since the Middle Ages.

Chief witness was seventy-seven-year-old Mr. T. R. Daly, who says girls are ruined in the dance hall, that the morals there rival those of Sodom and Gomorrah.

As he repeated his accusations before Assistant Charity Commissioner Mr. W. F. Fox, he was asked by the counsel for the dance hall trustees:

"Are you not a trouble-seeking, interfering, scandal-mongering, dishonest old man?"
Mr. Daly: To be sure I am standing for God and truth. . . .
He got no further. He was howled down.

Half the village attended the "trial." They crowded round the solicitors and clerks in the "orchestra stalls," bulged round the doorway and sat on the floor.

A cheer greeted Mr. Daly as his solicitor Mr. H. H. Norris. called him to make his charges

ABOVE: *Daily Mirror,* 30 April 1938; BELOW: a newspaper cartoon, and RIGHT: Thomas Henry Bennett of Cobham Court, Master of Fox Hounds and the man who gave the land on which the village hall was built.

## COBHAM & DISTRICT HORTICULTURAL SOCIETY

### *Annual Summer Show*
Open to Cobham and Cobham Postal District
(exception Class 38 open to a 10 mile radius)

### *Schedule of Prizes*
*of the*

# *45th Exhibition*
*to be held on*

## *Wednesday, July 20th, 1932*
*at*

## *Fairmile Court*
(by kind invitation of SIR MALCOLM & LADY McALPINE)

*President :*
LT.-COL. C. A. GORDON CLARK, C.M.G., D.S.O.

*Vice-Presidents :*
LORD EBBISHAM      C. H. COMBE, ESQ.      W. J. FIRTH, ESQ.
A. L. LAZARUS, ESQ.      P. MACHIN, ESQ.
SIR MALCOLM McALPINE, K.B.E.      R. T. D. STONEHAM, ESQ.

*Hon. Treasurer :*
B. W. GOLDS, ESQ., Westminster Bank Ltd., Cobham.

*Secretary :*          *Hon. Auditor :*          *Asst. Secretary :*
MR. W. STADDON,      MR. A. HAMILTON          MR. J. HUNT
4, Stanley Villas,
Leigh Road, Cobham.

*Committee :*
*Chairman :* B. W. GOLDS.

MRS. KITCHING,      MRS. GOODBODY,      MISS PRIDHAM,
MESSRS. C. A. AYRES,      A. BREWER,      F. J. BRIGHT,      A. COBBETT,
F. H. CRIPPS, C. DENLY, F. DODSON, G. C. FARRANT, J. GIBBINS,
R. J. GILL, A. E. HULL, J. HUNT, A. KEMBER, W. W. LEUCHARS,
F. MANFIELD, C. PULLEN, G. RADFORD, C. E. READ.

ABOVE: The Savoy Cinema on the Portsmouth Road and LEFT:
programme; RIGHT: Cobham & District Horticultural Society — Summer
Show, 1932.

# FESTIVITIES

held in honour of

# The Coronation

of

His Gracious Majesty King George V.

ABOVE: Cricket on the Tilt Green, c1905; CENTRE: a walking match in Cobham organised by Mr Deacon of Pointers, c1905, and BELOW: from the Coronation programme of 1911.

# Great and Glorious

A guide book of the 1840s described Cobham as 'quite a model of a sequestered country hamlet' which 'must be very refreshing in its quietness to the many anglers who escape to it from the noise of London'. However, it was not only the anglers who were attracted to Cobham but, during the eighteenth and nineteenth centuries, a number of interesting and colourful personalities chose to make their homes in the village.

During 1794 and 1795 Francis Wrangham, the classical scholar and writer, served as curate for the Parish of Cobham and while here joined with his friend Basil Montagu in running a school, taking pupils at £200 per annum each. Sir James Mackintosh said of the school's prospectus that 'a boy thus educated will be a walking encyclopaedia'. At this period of his life Wrangham was a constant figure in London's intellectual society but, more important, Montagu and John Pinney, the son of a rich West Indian Merchant from Bristol, were great friends of the poet William Wordsworth, who sometimes joined them on their visits to Cobham and thereby formed a life long friendship with Wrangham.

About 1780 Dr John Trusler, an eccentric divine and writer, made his home in Cobham, probably near Chilbrook Farm, Downside. Trusler was the son of the proprietor of the public tea gardens at Marylebone and became a priest in 1759. He later established an acadamy for teaching oratory 'mechanically' but as it did not pay, he soon gave it up. He studied medicine and seems to have assumed a medical doctorate after a spell at Leyden University. In 1769 he instigated a successful business, by printing in imitation of handwriting, a collection of sermons which he sold for one shilling each, in order to save clergy both study and the trouble of transcription. He later moved to Bath where he died in 1820.

Trusler's *Practical Husbandry, or the Art of Farming with certainty of gain,* first published in 1780, refers to local farming methods and in particular, the methods of dead hedging that were in use in Cobham at that time.

Henry Skrine, the tourist and writer, was the grandson of Richard Skrine of Pyports. Henry was baptised at Cobham Church in 1755 and as 'Mr. Skrine the Tourist' he endured the dangers and discomforts of eighteenth century roads, to produce pioneer books on travelling in the wilder parts of Britain. He died at Walton on Thames in 1803 and is buried there.

Just across the road from Pyports, and adjoining the churchyard, stands a house now called Church Corner. This was the home of William Watts, the engraver, from 1814 until his death, shortly before his 100th birthday, in 1851. Although he lived to the year of the Great Exhibition, he distinctly remembered the news of the death of Wolfe at Quebec in 1759 and the accession of George III in 1760. He is buried in the churchyard only a few yards from his home.

Another 'celebrity' to reside at Cobham was Admiral Sir Graham Moore, brother of the more famous Sir John Moore. In 1804, Graham Moore had enriched himself with prize money from Spanish treasure ships captured off Cadiz, and this enabled him to purchase Brook Farm, Cobham in the following year. The estate had been advertised as 'a desirable freehold estate comprising a singularly elegant villa with roomy stabling . . . suited to the Villa, the Mansion or the Farm Ornee'. The house had been built in 1800 by Colonel Edward Letherland on the edge of ground enclosed from the Tilt Common. The building was demolished about 1926 and is now represented by Brook Farm Road.

Sir John Moore often visited his brother at Cobham and in 1807 he planted the oak tree which still stands in the garden of one of the houses in Oak Road. Graham Moore spent a good deal of time and money on his Cobham home and in 1825 wrote, 'In fine weather, and particularly in the early spring of the year, this place appears very beautiful in my eyes'.

Admiral Sir Graham Moore died at Brook Farm on 9 December 1826 and is buried in Cobham churchyard together with his wife and son.

Another distinguished naval personage, and a friend of Admiral Moore, was Sir William Hoste, who came to live in Pyports in about 1826. Early in his career, Hoste became known to the enemy as 'Young Nelson'. He had served under Nelson for five years and was present at the Battle of the Nile. He missed Trafalgar and later wrote that 'not to have been in the battle is enough to make one mad; but to have lost such as friend besides is really sufficient to almost overwhelm me'. At Cobham, Hoste was an enthusiastic gardener, taking a particular interest in flowers. He died in London in 1828 and has a statue to his memory in St Paul's Cathedral.

It was about this time that Karoline Bauer, mistress of Prince Leopold of Claremont, came to live at Heywood, the large white house on the Fairmile Common which is now the home of the American Community School. Leopold's wife, Charlotte, had died tragically in childbirth at Claremont, leaving him heartbroken. The remarkable resemblance of Karoline, an actress, to his late wife led Leopold to propose to her, but since marriage would have cost him his pension of £50,000 a year as widower of the Princess Royal, she was secretly installed in a house in Regent's Park. Some sort of marriage was arranged in 1829 and, on New Year's Eve, Karoline and her mother were installed at Heywood, which Leopold had bought in 1820.

Karoline was never happy there, describing the house as a 'solitary and gloomy villa'. Leopold would often drive over from Claremont for dinner but Karoline became bored with the relationship and her solitary life. She returned to the stage. In 1832 Leopold (then King of the Belgians) was married again to Louise, eldest daughter of Louis Phillipe.

In 1823, the young Caroline Molesworth came to live at Cobham Lodge, near Downside; her mother was the widow of Sir William Molesworth of Pencarrow in Cornwall. Lady Molesworth had inherited the house (designed by the Regency architect J.B. Papworth) under the will of General Felix Buckley, a veteran of the battle of Culloden, and her daughter continued to live there after her mother's death in 1842, and until her own in 1872.

Caroline Molesworth kept a comprehensive account of the meteorology, flora, fauna and natural phenomena of the district. These notes were published after her death in *The Cobham Journals*. Although much of the information is of a scientific nature, there are references to local events such as 'a peculiar vibration, believed to be an earthquake' in 1830. In 1840 'a huricane . . . blowing down trees at Cobham Park and Pains Hill' is recorded and later there are references to wild geese, snipe, red throated divers and great crested grebe in the vicinity and 'a bittern shot in Cobham Park'.

Caroline Molesworth was noted for her kindness and generosity and 'with a character for ecentricity not wholly unmerited, she was still greately respected in her own neighbourhood'.

In the middle years of the nineteenth century, the artist Spencer Stanhope came to live in Cobham, first at Norwood Farm and then at the house now called Benfleet Hall in Green Lane, which was designed for him by the noted architect Philip Webb, whose previous commission had been The Red House at Bexley for William Morris. Stanhope was associated with the Pre-Raphaelite Brotherhood and had worked with Rossetti and the others on the famous Oxford Union murals.

At Cobham, Spencer Stanhope entertained Burne Jones and the two artists used local scenery in some of their pictures. One painting in particular, by Spencer Stanhope, entitled 'The Mill Pond' clearly shows the mill at Cobham. George Frederick Watts, the artist, came here with his young bride Ellen Terry from Esher, where they were staying with friends. It is recorded that Ellen, beautiful but bored, let loose her mass of golden hair till it swept the drawing room floor, much to the horror of the older ladies present.

A near neighbour of Spencer Stanhope was Mrs Theresa Earle, a prolific writer and keen gardener chiefly known for her books in the series *Pot Pouri from a Surrey Garden*. Mrs Earle's home was Woodlands, Green Lane and the garden is now occupied by the road called Earleswood. She was the aunt of architect Edwin Lutyens' wife. Lutyens first met her at Munstead Wood, near Goldalming, the home of his partner, gardener Gertrude Jekyll. Mrs Earle was renowned for her hospitality and delicious food and it is almost certain that both Lutyens and Miss Jekyll would have visited her at Woodlands. The author Henry James was another visitor.

Pyports seems to have had more than its fair share of distinguished residents. During the 1860s the house was occupied by Charles Dines, an assistant to the great builder of the Victorian age, George Cubitt. In about 1870, the house became the residence of the Lushington family.

Stephen Lushington of Ockham Park had been a High Court Judge and had, as a barrister, advised both Queen Caroline and Lady Byron on their matrimonial problems. Stephen's son Vernon, also a lawyer, was both a Christian Socialist and a member of the Positivist Society which propogated what Vernon called 'the beautiful and true Religion of Humanity'. Through his involvement with both the Positivists and the Christian Socialists Vernon became closely connected with a number of the leading men and women of his day including John Ruskin, George Eliot, Charles Kingsley, Mrs Gaskell, Thomas Hardy, Matthew Arnold, Leslie Stephen and F. D. Maurice.

It was Vernon's involvement with Maurice at the Working Mens College in London that brought him into contact with Dante Gabriel Rossetti, the artist and through Vernon, Rossetti was introduced to Burne-Jones, with whom he formed a long partnership as a member of the Pre-Raphaelite group.

Vernon's wife, Jane, was painted by Rossetti in the year of her marriage and his daughter's portraits were executed by Holman Hunt and Arthur Hughes. Hunt came to Cobham on at least one occasion when Vernon's eldest daughter, Katherine, was married to Leopold Maxse, the owner and editor of the *National Review*. The two had met through Mrs Leslie Stephen, who became a second mother to Vernon's daughter after Jane's death. Mrs Stephen's daughter Virginia was to become known to the world as Virginia Woolf, the novelist. Virginia was a close friend of Kitty Lushington during their early years, and both she and her sister probably stayed at Pyports during their childhood. Sir Leslie Stephen recorded staying with his family at Pyports in 1888.

Margaret Lushington married Stephen Massingberd of Gunby Hall, Lincolnshire in 1895 and it was a cousin of the bridegroom, the young Ralph Vaughan Williams who played the organ at St Andrew's parish church. Other recorded visitors to Pyports are Matthew Arnold, the philosopher Dr J. H. Bridges, and A. J. Munby, the barrister and poet. Another visitor was almost certainly George Meredith, who lived near Cobham and who was a great friend of the Maxse family. Meredith certainly visited Cobham during his walking expeditions from Copsham Cottage between Esher and Oxshott.

Vernon Lushington's passion for helping the deprived was demonstrated by his contributions to the new Cobham Village Hall and to the local schools. The barn at Pyports was used as a rehearsal room for a local orchestra under the supervision of his youngest daughter Susan.

Vernon Lushington had been a graduate of Trinity College, Cambridge where he had been a member of a select society called the Cambridge Apostles. Membership brought him into close contact with the two greatest minds of the age — J.S. Mill and Thomas Carlyle.

A later member of the Cambridge Apostles was Walter Leaf, whose father Charles had purchased the Painshill estate in 1872, and it was there that Walter spent a part of his early life. C.J. Leaf, a London merchant, had previously lived at Harrow, where Walter had been educated. Walter won a classical scholarship to Trinity College and later became a Fellow. He eventually abandoned his intended career at the bar and entered the family firm. He went on to distinguish himself in the banking world and in 1926, as President of the International Chamber of Commerce, he made an important and successful visit to Germany with a view to economic reconciliation. However, Walter Leaf's reputation rests chiefly on his work as a Greek scholar. He worked with Andrew Lang to produce a translation of Homer's *Iliad* and a later edition of his became the best edition in the English language. He published a number of other books and later he and his wife became close friends of Virginia Woolf. Walter Leaf died in Torquay in 1927.

Cobham's literary connections continued into the twentieth century and Daphne du Maurier stayed for a short time as a child at Slyfield House. Cobham is featured in H.G. Wells' *War Of The Worlds* and Conan Doyle based his *Adventure Of The Speckled Band* at Stoke D'Abernon, the Plough being the model for the inn where Holmes and Watson stayed.

One other noted resident of the early twentieth century was David Lloyd George, who lived at Upper Court between Cobham and Esher. Bought for him in 1919, several important meetings were held at the house, then known as The Firs, and many important figures of the day visited.

Cobham has continued to be a popular residential area with the large areas of housing that were developed on the Fairmile, and elsewhere, between two world wars. Today it is film actors and 'pop stars' who put their stamp on the community.

Cobham High Street by J. Hassell 1827, looking towards River Hill; on the right, the Fox and Hounds and on the left, the Crown. The building in the centre distance is now La Capana.

LEFT: Church Street, Cobham, by J. Hassell, 1822, looking towards the church; RIGHT: Admiral Sir Graham Moore of Brook Farm, by Sir Thomas Lawrence; CENTRE: the oak tree planted in the grounds of Brook Farm by Sir John Moore in 1807; and BELOW: Brook Farm, by J. Hassell, 1822.

113

Mrs. Vernon Lushington from the portrait by D.G. Rossetti painted in the year of her marriage.

ABOVE LEFT: Cobham Lodge, home of Miss Caroline Molesworth, and RIGHT: Pyports, home of Sir William Hoste, Vernon Lushington and Samuel Bradnack. LEFT: Vernon Lushington of Pyports; RIGHT: R. Spencer Stanhope from the photograph by C.L. Dodgson (Lewis Carroll).

LEFT: Mrs Earle, the writer, in the garden of her home at Woodlands, Fairmile Lane, and RIGHT: David Lloyd George from the portrait by W. Orpen. He lived at the house now called Upper Court on the Fairmile, seen BELOW: in water colour when it was The Firs and home of General Sir Thomas William Brotherton GCB, a hero of the Peninsula War, buried at Cobham Church.

# Change and Challenge

At the opening of the nineteenth century, Cobham was a small rural community with a population of 1,200. One fifth of the population was engaged in agriculture and the total number of occupied houses in the village was only 208. By the end of the century, the population had risen to almost 3,000. The Cobham of 1900 was different in appearance to that of 1800 and the last fifty years of the century probably saw far more changes in the local community than had ever been witnessed before. Nationally, low wages had led to a decrease in the number of people working on the land and the railways brought an increase in travel and a new industrial boom. In Cobham, as in many other places, much of the farmland was replaced by low-cost housing development and gradually the separate communities of Street Cobham, Church Cobham and Tilt Cobham merged into one.

Sweeping changes were brought by the enclosure of the old open fields of the parish into neat, rectangular hedged fields. Enclosure, which was designed to make better use of the land and increase crop production, meant a reallocation of the many small land holdings in the parish and was often done at the expense of both the smallholder and the poorer folk who depended greatly on their rights in the common land.

A different sort of attack on the commons had been led by Gerrard Winstanley in the seventeenth century and in the sixteenth century, a large part of Cobham had been enclosed for a period as part of King Henry VIII's new Chase of Hampton Court, which extended out through Esher and Cobham and which included Painshill. The Chase, or deer park, was enclosed by a fence and dry ditch and there were six 'sawtrees', or deer leaps, in the fence, so constructed that the deer could enter but not escape. Gates were constructed for horses and carts to pass through and there were stiles for those on foot. Some of the timber for the fence was cut in Cobham and a postern gate was constructed at 'Cobham Fold' which was probably on the Fairmile Common. Forest law prevailed within the chase and the whole exercise was greatly resented by local people, who were put to considerable hardship. The fence was removed soon after the King's death, but the area is still technically a Royal chase and subject to all former laws.

A certain amount of enclosure had taken place in Cobham before the eighteenth century, but this had usually been by mutual agreement between the parties involved. However, in 1779 the lord of the manor, Thomas Page, obtained a private Act of Parliament for 'dividing and inclosing the common and open fields within the parish'. This was one of the earliest enclosure acts in Surrey and dealt with the cultivated strips which had dwindled in extent from 481¾ acres in 1598 to 370 acres at the time of the Act. The common land and waste ground were enclosed by a later act in 1793. According to this there were several large open commons, heath and marsh, and wastelands in Cobham, and across these were to be laid new roads not less than forty feet wide, and no trees were to be planted on either side nearer to each other than fifty yards. Certain areas of land were to be set aside for gravel pits, for the construction and maintenance of the new roads. Some of the roads constructed can be seen nowadays in the long straight stretches of the Portsmouth Road, Fairmile Lane, Stoke Road, Bookham Common Road and Horsley Road.

Throughout the last century, communities such as Cobham were dominated by those who owned the land. The enclosure of the old open fields helped bring into existence a number of compact farms and estates such as Cobham Park, Cobham Court, Eaton Farm and Leighill Farm. Cobham Park was the home of the Combe family while the Pages and later the Deacons lived at Pointers. Leighill Farm was owned by the Bennett family who had been in Cobham for several generations. When Thomas Bennett died in 1878, his sons Thomas Henry and Theodore Joseph inherited the Leigh Hill Farm estate which dominated a large part of Cobham north of the High Street. T. H. Bennett later acquired Cobham Court and became a popular Master of Fox Hounds. In 1883 a large part of the Leigh Hill estate was sold off as building plots and is now represented by Anyards Road, Copse Road, Hogshill Lane and Cedar Road. In 1880, Eaton Farm had been sold as a building estate, and gradually the Fairmile became a popular residential area. A number of older houses such as Fairmile Court have survived, although their gardens have given way to modern housing development.

There were a number of abortive attempts to bring the railway into Cobham in the middle years of the nineteenth century, and several prominent local residents voiced their hopes that this would bring an increase in both trade and development in the area. If the railway promoters had succeeded and a railway station had been built on the site of Oakdene Parade, Cobham today would be a very different place.

Increasing population and development brought a growing concern for public amenities. The requirement of local administration developed far beyond the capacity of the parish Vestry, whose rating powers were limited to the relief of the poor and the maintenance of the parish church. Policing continued to be the responsibility of the parish until the formation of the Surrey Constabulary. The present Cobham police station was opened in the early 1900s and in 1947 Cobham was taken into the Metropolitan District.

From the middle of the last century, successive acts created a welter of District Boards with rate-raising power for particular objects such as roads, drains, schools, street lighting and burials. The Boards were often dominated by local landowners and a thoughtful, benevolent squire would mean a well cared-for community.

As in most other village communities, schooling in Cobham had been largely a charitable affair. James Fox, lord of the manor, had endowed a charity school for forty children in the 1720s. A limited education was also provided for the workhouse children and, later in the nineteenth century, the owner of the local brickfields, J.E. Cook, provided education for his workers and their families. In 1833 a National School was built on the Tilt and the building later became a Parish Room and was used for a while as a soup kitchen. It later became the village fire station. The parochial schools in Cedar Road were built in 1860 by Miss Combe of Cobham Park in memory of her brother. An infants school was built in Hogshill Lane and the Secondary School in Lockhart Road was opened in 1958.

Provision of a local fire engine became a matter of public concern in 1890 following a serious fire at Cobham Court. A letter to the *Surrey Advertiser* revealed that Cobham had 'once possessed a fire engine that had been allowed to rot unused in a field'. It was not until 1898, after a further serious fire, that Charles Combe of Cobham Park offered to provide the village with one that would cost him £500.

The new Merryweather was handed over at a grand ceremony at Cobham Park in 1899. It was christened with champagne by Mrs Combe and nine visiting brigades joined in a spectacular display, throwing jets of water into the lake while the Cobham Brass Band played. The engine was soon put to good use in dealing with fires at Stoke D'Abernon and Cobham Court. It remained stationed at the Tilt until the 1960s and the present Painshill Fire Station was opened some years later.

In 1885 Charles Combe had presented some land on the Tilt to the Cobham Burial Board for the site of the present cemetery. Combe had also been instrumental in organising a public meeting in 1866 to ascertain the desirability of bringing the mains of the Leatherhead Water Company into Cobham and, two years later, he chaired a public meeting to consider 'the proprietry of introducing gas into the parish'. The Cobham Gas Light & Coke Company was formed two years later, its premises near Cobham Bridge. Street lighting was introduced in 1899 and mains drainage followed a few years after that.

Health and social welfare went hand in hand with the town's development but were originally largely matters of local charity backed by parish support. A Sanitary Committee had been established in 1873 consisting of Messrs Cook, Bennett, Combe, Ashby and Dallen and the following year it was empowered to spend not more than £50 'to take steps for the repression of scarlet fever in the parish'.

Cobham had a number of charitable institutions such as Coal and Clothing Clubs during the late nineteenth century, and the various Friendly Societies, which had been formed largely as a result of the new Poor Law, enabled many of the poorer people to receive some sort of medical attention. A Parish Nurse was later provided and supported by voluntary subscriptions and a 'Cobham Nurse Fund & Home' was led by the Dowager Countess of Ellesmere. A Nurse's Home was built on the Portsmouth Road and the present Cottage Hospital was built in 1905 and opened by HRH the Duchess of Albany in June of that year and enlarged in 1913. Voluntary medical assistance was also provided by the St John Ambulance Brigade, formed in 1906 following a series of lectures at Downside by Dr J. Kitching. Through the assistance of Sir Henry Samuelson, then living at Hatchford Park, a hand-wheeled basket ambulance was acquired for use at the hospital.

When A.J. Munby visited Cobham in 1861 he found the 'Cobham Reading Rooms' which had been opened five years previously. There were three classes of subscribers: 'the trades people and folk of the better sort', the 'working men' and a class for young men. History was then the favourite subject. A Parish Library was opened in 1886 and received a gift of books from the poet Matthew Arnold. For many years a local library was housed in the Village Hall and the present Cobham Branch Library in Hollyhedge Road was opened after the war, having been converted from an ARP cleansing station.

The creation of the various district boards and the numerous charitable and voluntary organisations eventually produced a chaos of overlapping authorities, all acting independently of each other. To simplify the system, County Councils were established in 1888 to administer County-wide matters, and District Councils in 1895 to deal with matters of local concern. Cobham was originally in the Epsom Rural District, but in 1933 it was annexed to Esher Urban District. In 1974 the Urban Districts of Esher and Walton & Weybridge were merged to form the present Elmbridge Borough.

**WHEREAS** there are within the Manor of *Cobham*, other- Preamble. wife *Coveham*, in the Parifh of *Cobham*, in the County of *Surrey*, feveral large Open Commons, Heaths, and Marfh and Wafte Lands, which contain by Eftimation about One thoufand Seven hundred Acres:

And whereas *Thomas Page*, Efquire, is Lord of the faid Manor; and he, together with the Vicar of the faid Parifh, in refpect of his Glebe Land, *Henry Perkin Wefton*, Efquire, Impropriator of the Great and Small Tythes

Part of the title page from the Enclosure Act of 1793.

*Cobham, Surrey.*

PARTICULARS, AND CONDITIONS OF SALE,
OF SIX PIECES OF
UNINCLOSED FREEHOLD LAND,

Being Part of the " Commons, Heaths, and Marſh and Waſte Lands,"

In the PARISH of *COBHAM*, within the COUNTY of *SURREY*,

Directed to be divided and incloſed by virtue of an Act of Parliament paſſed in the Year 1793, which are allotted and ſet out by the Commiſſioners appointed by the ſaid Act, agreable to the Powers contained therein, towards defraying the Charges and Expences of paſſing and carrying the ſaid Act into execution:

Which will be SOLD by AUCTION, at the *George* Inn, at *Cobham-Street*, on MONDAY the 14th Day of *JULY*, 1794, at Twelve o'Clock, in Six Lots,

## By Mr. *YOUNG*.

### LOT I.

*In Fair Mile Common.* A PARCEL of LAND, containing 40 Acres (more or leſs), being Part of *Fair Mile Common*, called *The Bottom*, lying open, and adjoining to the Commons in the Manor of *Eſher* and *Milburne*; ſituate on the South-Eaſt Side of, and adjoining to, the Turnpike Road leading from *Kingſton* to *Guildford*.
The Purchaſer of this Lot to fence and incloſe the ſame at his own Expence, on the North-Weſt, againſt the ſaid Turnpike Road; on the North-Eaſt and Eaſt againſt the ſaid Commons in the Manor of *Eſher* and *Milburne*; and on the South-Weſt and Weſt againſt the open Common belonging to the ſaid Manor of *Cobham*.

### LOT II.

*In Old Common.* A PARCEL of LAND, containing 14 Acres (more or leſs), being Part of the Common called the *Old Common*, bounded on Parts of the North and Part at the Eaſt by *Norwood Manor Farm*; on the remaining Part of the Eaſt, on the South, and on the Weſt, by the open Common belonging to the ſaid Manor of *Cobham*.
The Purchaſer of this Lot to fence and incloſe the ſame at his own Expence, on all Parts and Sides where it adjoins the open Common belonging to the ſaid Manor of *Cobham*.

### LOT III.

*In the Tilt.* A PARCEL of LAND, as now flaked out, containing 3 Acres (more or leſs), being Part of the Common called *the Tilt*, ſituate near the South-Eaſt Corner thereof, and oppoſite to the *Poor-Houſe*.
The Purchaſer of this Lot to fence and incloſe the ſame at his own Expence, on the Eaſt, South, and Weſt Sides thereof.

### LOT IV.

*In the Tilt.* A PARCEL of LAND, as now flaked out, containing 3 Acres (more or leſs), being Part of the ſaid Common called *the Tilt*; ſituate on the North Side of, and adjoining to, Lot III.
The Purchaſer of this Lot to fence and incloſe the ſame at his own Expence, on the Eaſt, South, and Weſt Sides thereof.

### LOT V.

*In the Tilt.* A PARCEL of LAND, as now flaked out, containing 3 Acres (more or leſs), being Part of the ſaid Common called *the Tilt*, and lying between the new Road through the ſaid *Tilt* on the North, and Lot IV. on the South.
The Purchaſer of this Lot to fence and incloſe the ſame at his own Expence, on the North againſt the ſaid Road, on the South againſt Lot IV. and on the Weſt againſt the open Tilt.

### LOT VI.

*In the Tilt.* A PARCEL of LAND, as now flaked out, containing 3 Acres (more or leſs), being Part of the ſaid Common called *the Tilt*; ſituate near the Lane leading to *Stoke D'Abernon*, and on the South Side of the new Road through the ſaid *Tilt*.
The Purchaſer of this Lot to fence and incloſe the ſame at his own Expence, on the Eaſt, South, Weſt, and North Sides thereof.

By Order of { WILLIAM YOUNG, *Chancery-lane* }
{ GEORGE SMALLPIECE, *Stoke*, next *Guildford*, } Commiſſioners appointed by
{ JOHN MIDDLETON, *Lambeth*, } the ſaid Act.

Mr. INGELOW, the Surveyor to the ſaid Incloſure, and Mr. CRAWTER, at *Cobham*, will ſhew the Lots, of whom printed PARTICULARS may be had: Alſo at the White Lion and George Inns, *Cobham*; of Mr. BRAY, *Great Ruſſel Street*, Clerk to the Commiſſioners; at *Garraway's*, and of the Commiſſioners.

### CONDITIONS OF SALE

I. THE higheſt Bidder to be the Purchaſer; and if any Diſpute ariſe between Two or more Bidders, the Lot to be put up again, and reſold.
II. No Perſon to advance leſs than £2 at each Bidding.
III. Each Purchaſer to pay down immediately to Mr. YOUNG a Depoſit of £20 *per Cent.* in Part of the Purchaſe-Money, and ſign an Agreement for Payment of the Remainder on or before the Third Day of *Auguſt*, next.
IV. The Purchaſer of each Lot to have a proper Receipt agreeable to the Act of Parliament, at his own Expence, on Payment of the Remainder of the Purchaſe-Money, according to the Third Condition; and to be entitled to the Poſſeſſion from the Time of completing the Purchaſe.
V. There being a Duty on all Sales of Eſtates, &c. of Threepence-halfpenny in the Pound, to be levied on the Buyer or Seller as may be thought moſt proper; the Lots contained in this Particular are to be ſold, reſpect to the Buyer's paying the ſaid Duty over and above the Sum the ſaid Lots ſhall ſell for.
Laſtly, if the Purchaſer ſhall neglect or fail to comply with the above Conditions, the Depoſit-Money ſhall be forfeited; and the Commiſſioners be at full Liberty to re-ſell the ſaid Lot; and the Deficiency, if any there ſhall be by ſuch Second Sale, together with all Charges attending the ſame, ſhall be made good by the Defaulter at this preſent Sale.

---

LEFT: Sale particulars of land sold after the 1793 Act, and RIGHT: part of the Old Common, c1910. BELOW: Sale particulars for land in Anyards Road, 1883.

---

ELIGIBLE FREEHOLD BUILDING LAND
AT
# COBHAM, SURREY.

Particulars and Conditions of Sale
OF
SEVERAL PLOTS OF VALUABLE
## FREEHOLD
# BUILDING LAND,
SITUATE
*Fronting the High Portsmouth Road,*
AND CONTINUING ALONG
THE NEW ANYARD'S ROAD
TO
CHURCH COBHAM;

The Property is admirably situate close to the Church, Post Office, &c., within a short distance of the proposed

RAILWAY STATION ON THE NEW KINGSTON & GUILDFORD LINE,

And will be offered with easy arrangements as to completion of purchase, rendering it desirable for small capitalists seeking to possess a Freehold Property.

FOR SALE BY AUCTION, BY

# JOHN DAWSON & SON

*AT THE WHITE LION HOTEL, COBHAM,*

On WEDNESDAY, the 14th day of March, 1883,

AT 3 FOR 4 O'CLOCK PRECISELY, IN LOTS.

Particulars with Plan and Conditions of Sale may be obtained of JAMES BELL, Esq., Solicitor, High Street, Kingston-on-Thames, and of

JOHN DAWSON & SON,
Land and Auction Offices,
Surbiton, Kingston-on-Thames, and 1, Lancaster Place, Strand, W.C.

# COBHAM, SURREY.

### PARTICULARS
#### OF
### A Very Compact and Desirable
## FREEHOLD
# BUILDING ESTATE,
##### KNOWN AS
## EATON FARM,
#### OCCUPYING AN ELEVATED POSITION, COMMANDING EXTENSIVE VIEWS,

Situate about four miles from the Esher and Leatherhead Stations on the London and South-Western Railway; a very select neighbourhood, in proximity to Claremont, and surrounded by lands belonging to J. A. Radcliffe, Esq., Sir H. Moore. — Bennett, Esq., Col. Wood, — Keys, Esq., J. Early Cook, Esq., and H. Jupp, Esq.,

##### COMPRISING
## A FARM HOUSE,
##### WITH
### GARDENS, STABLING, AGRICULTURAL BUILDINGS,
#### AND
### *Enclosures of Undulating Meadow & Arable Land,*

The Estate comprises altogether about

# 144 ACRES,
##### THE WHOLE
#### ADMIRABLY ADAPTED FOR SUB DIVISION FOR BUILDING PURPOSES,
#### WITH POSSESSION.

WHICH WILL BE SOLD BY AUCTION, BY MESSRS.

## NORTON, TRIST, WATNEY & Co.,

**At the Mart, Tokenhouse Yard, E.C.**

On FRIDAY, 21st MAY, 1880, at Two o'clock precisely,

**In Two Lots.**

# SURREY.

Particulars, Views, Plan and Conditions of Sale

OF THE IMPORTANT

# Freehold Residential Property
##### KNOWN AS
## "The Knowle Hill Estate,"
### COBHAM,
##### COMPRISING A
## MODERATE SIZED MANSION

In the Italian style of architecture, surrounded by very

### *Lovely old Gardens and Grounds,*
##### AND A
### WELL-TIMBERED UNDULATING PARK

With excellent Lodge Entrance.

### EXTENSIVE STABLING,

Very **AMPLE FARM BUILDINGS**, AGENT'S HOUSE, FIVE COTTAGES, LAUNDRY, GLASS HOUSES, KITCHEN GARDEN, ORCHARD, &c., the whole forming a

### MOST COMPACT AND VALUABLE ESTATE,
##### EXTENDING TO ABOUT
# 115 Acres,
##### AND POSSESSING
### IMPORTANT FRONTAGES TO MAIN ROADS.

Portions of which could be immediately dealt with for Building Purposes if desired.

### POSSESSION ON COMPLETION OF THE PURCHASE.
#### *MESSRS.*

## ALEX. H. TURNER & CO.

Are instructed to offer the above Valuable Estate by Auction,

AT THE MART, LONDON, E.C.

On TUESDAY, the 28th day of JUNE, 1904,

AT TWO O'CLOCK

(*Unless previously disposed of by Private Treaty*).

LEFT: Sale particulars for Eaton Farm in 1880, and RIGHT: for Knowle Hill Estate in 1904. BELOW: Anyards Road, c1905.

ABOVE: First house built in **INSET**: Freelands Road, c1904. BELOW: Surfacing Anyards Road near the Village Hall, c1903. (In the right background, the Tartar Fields, now covered by Tartar Road, Canada Road and Lockhart Road.)

ABOVE: Laying drainage pipes in Cobham, c1905. LEFT: HRH the
Duchess of Albany at the opening of Cobham Cottage Hospital, and
RIGHT: the new hospital.

Incorporated by the Cobham Gas Act, 1899.

# THE
# COBHAM GAS COMPANY.

*Under the above Act of Parliament, power has been obtained to purchase the Gas Works formerly owned by the*

## COBHAM GAS LIGHT & COKE CO., Ltd., established in 1870.

CAPITAL £15,000, in 1,500 Shares of £10 each.

Issue at Par of

# 1,500 ORDINARY SHARES OF £10 EACH

**(Ranking for Dividend up to Ten per cent. per annum).**

## A MINIMUM DIVIDEND OF 4 PER CENT. IS GUARANTEED FOR THREE YEARS.

PAYMENTS—£2 per Share on application.
£2 ,, ,, on the 28th May.
£2 ,, ,, ,, 30th July.
£2 ,, ,, ,, 1st October.
£2 ,, ,, ,, 3rd December.
———
£10

THE LIABILITY ON THE SHARES IS LIMITED TO £10 PER SHARE.
The Borrowing powers are limited by Section 8 to one-third of the Share Capital.

### The Company's Bankers.
PARR'S BANK⬛⬛⬛⬛ LIMITED, COBHAM, SURREY.

*The List will OPEN on WEDNESDAY, the 21st day of MARCH, and will CLOSE on or before SATURDAY, the 24th MARCH, 1900*

The Directors give notice that they are prepared to receive applications **at par for 1,500 Ordinary Shares of £10 each (ranking for dividend up to 10 per cent.),** being the Company's authorised capital under section 6 of the Cobham Gas Act, 1899.

The carbonizing capacity of the recently acquired Gas Works equalled 10,000,000 (ten million) cubic feet of gas per annum. Owing to the smallness of the works and mains, the former Company was unable, in many instances, to meet the demands for gas; consequently additional buildings and plant are being erected. The old mains have been replaced by larger sizes and new mains are being laid over a very considerable new area, as shewn on the accompanying map. This will ensure more economical working and enable the Company to supply 20,000,000 (twenty million) cubic feet of gas per annum.

The Cobham Gas Light and Coke Company, Limited, was established in 1870. After materially reducing the price of gas and expending considerable sums out of profits for the improvement and extension of the works, the Company for 26 years paid dividends on their Capital averaging $4\frac{1}{4}$ per cent. In the year ending June 30th, 1899, the profit made was equivalent to a dividend of $6\frac{3}{4}$ per cent. The Directors believe that, with the improvements now made and contemplated, and the anticipated increase of business, the Company will in due course be able to pay the maximum dividend of 10 per cent. on the present issue.

Prospectus of the Cobham Gas Company, 1900.

## COBHAM NURSE FUND.

*Committee of Management*: Mrs. Arnold, Miss Blunt, Mrs. Earley Cook, Mrs. Deacon, Dowager Countess of Ellesmere, Hon. Lady Grey, Mrs. Lushington.

*Ex-officio Members of Committee*: Rev. C. B. Young, A. Hooley, Esq., R. Smith, Esq.

*Treasurer*: Dowager Countess of Ellesmere.

*Secretary*: Mrs. Lushington.

This Fund is maintained by public subscription, and has been raised for the purpose of supplying the services of a Trained Nurse to the sick and aged poor among the labouring classes in the parish.

All applications for the services of the nurse must be made to the Medical Officer attending the patient, who will issue the order for the attendance of the nurse, on a form provided for the purpose.

No gratuity or payment should be offered to the nurse, who will provide her own board. But tradesmen and others, who can afford it, when profiting by the use of the nurse, will be expected to make a donation to the fund according to their means. If the nurse is required to sit up at night an extra charge of 1/6 will be made for each night.

### RATES.

6d. for each ordinary daily visit of about an hour.

1/- for each day when more than one visit is paid, or where one visit entails three or four hours' attendance.

2/- will be charged when the nurse attends day and night, for each such attendance.

1/6 for each night's attendance when she attends at night only.

Nurse Dann is furnished with a card of these printed rules, to show to those persons to whom they are intended to apply.

### REPORT.

The Committee in laying their report before the Subscribers for the past year, have much pleasure in stating that this charity maintains its usefulness in the parish, and that Nurse Dann has discharged her duties to their entire satisfaction.

They are also glad to be able to lay before the subscribers a large list of supporters, but notwithstanding this, they find that their working expenses have slightly exceeded the income of the past year, and had it not been for the small surplus balance in hand from the previous year, there would have been a deficit.

The small balances annually brought forward have been steadily diminishing, and the Committee have also to regret the loss of a valued subscriber. They would therefore urgently appeal to their fellow-parishioners, in the hope of obtaining a few more names to the list of subsribers, so as to insure an income of not less than £110 per annum to carry on the work.

A Collector will be sent round for subscriptions during the next fortnight.

ABOVE: Cobham Nurses' Home, c1905, next to the Cobham Village Club, and BELOW: details of Cobham Nurse Fund from the Parish Magazine, 1886.

ABOVE: Cobham Central School — Form III — April 1931; CENTRE: Cobham's First Fire Engine, 1899; BELOW: Cobham Tilt and the Fire Station, c1905.

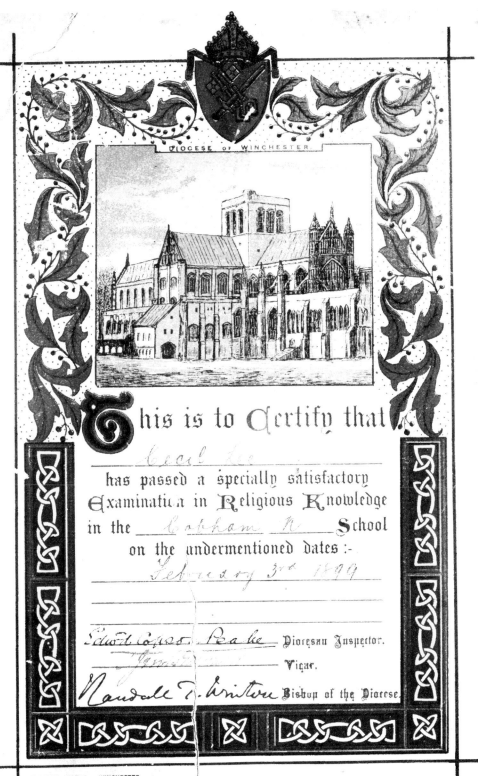

DIOCESE OF WINCHESTER

This is to Certify that

*Cecil Lee*

has passed a specially satisfactory Examination in Religious Knowledge in the *Cobham N.* School on the undermentioned dates :—

*February 3rd 1899*

*Edwd Capes Peake* Diocesan Inspector.

_____ Vicar.

*Randall T. Winton* Bishop of the Diocese.

Certificate presented to Cecil Lee from Cobham School in 1899.

ABOVE: Cobham High Street, c1910, looking towards the junction with
Between Streets and Anyards Road, INSET: trade token of Thomas King —
1667, and BELOW: Daniel Dallen's Steam Mill in Hollyhedge Road.

# *Private Enterprise*

Until the end of the nineteenth century, the trades and industries of Cobham were generally tied to the agricultural nature of the district and to the specific needs of the community.

In the seventeenth century, during a period when copper coinage was short, two Cobham tradesmen, Thomas King and Francis Tyrill issued their own token coinage.

Tanning was then a local industry for in 1609 Charles Collyns, Cobham tanner was indicted for petty larceny and punished by a whipping. Another local tanner in 1652 was Francis Sutton. In 1737 a property in Cobham was known as Tan House and this may have been the property now known as Cedar House.

A small group of buildings at the rear of La Capanna on River Hill were formerly known as Fellmongers Yard, a fellmonger being a dealer in skins and, in 1716, a glover called James Acklyn lived here.

The various county directories of the last century give a clearer indication of the sort of trades to be found in Cobham then. These tended to cater chiefly for local need and there was little manufactory on a large scale, save for milling and brewing.

Daniel Dallen opened the steam flour mill in Hollyhedge Road, on a site next to the present library, in the middle of the last century and set up home in Holly Lodge, a large eighteenth century house that formerly stood in the High Street on the site of Holly Parade.

The High Street at this time consisted of little more than Holden's Forge, Foster's Diary and a few houses. The artist J. Hassell has left us an interesting picture of a half timbered building that stood on the site later occupied by the Gammons building, and now replaced by Standard Property House. Church Street was the commercial centre of the village and here there were a stationer, butcher, grocer, draper, milliner and seedsman. Eldred Ledger, the watchmaker, known locally as 'Tickety' had his premises in the building now housing 'Phoenix', the dress shop.

In 1857, George Brown of Chertsey purchased the premises now occupied by 'Katie James' and set up business as a saddle and harness maker. In 1859 he was described as 'Saddler and Harness Maker, Stable Furnisher & Rope, Line and Twine Maker'. His business prospered and he purchased adjoining land on which he built new premises which, until quite recently, were owned by his descendants and known as 'Brown's Sports Shop'.

In 1888, the *Parish Magazine* included advertisements for W. Harding's Livery Stables at the White Lion Hotel Yard — 'Broughams, Landaus and Open Flys always in Readiness'; Joseph Hutchinson — 'Corn, Seed, Flour & Coal Merchant'; James Lynn — 'Family Butcher'; F. Holden — 'Whitesmith & Smiths Work in all its branches'; C. Souter — 'Fancy Stationer and Newsagent'; and T.C. Andrew — 'Cigar and Tobacco Stores, Hair Dresser and Ornamental Hair Worker'.

In the latter part of the century, brickmaking became an important local industry and there were two brickfields on the border of Cobham and Oxshott. The smaller field belonged to H.W. Scriven of Tudor Court, Fairmile Park Road, a strong nonconformist and staunch teetotaller. His brickfield occupied some five acres of ground alongside Knipp Hill and was in production about forty years, turning out 1,500 hand-made bricks per man-day.

Scriven's temperance activities led him to purchase the Griffin Inn at the top of Knipp Hill and close it down. His business closed down in 1939, largely due to the shortage of clay and difficulties over labour. The site was purchased and levelled by a Mr Goldsmidt and is now occupied by the Pony Chase estate.

The larger of the brickfields belonged to John Earley Cook, who came to Cobham in the 1860s. He purchased the Knowle Hill estate and built the house which, until recently, formed part of the Schiff Hospital. Cook's brickfield lay next to Littleheath and occupied about thirty acres.

J.E. Cook was a colourful personality, loved and respected by his workers but considered a rather difficult and obstinate man by others in the community. In 1885 he was elected Master of the Worshipful Company of Carpenters of London.

In the middle years of the last century Cook had been an objector to various plans to bring the railway into the centre of Cobham. However, in 1883, he sold part of his brick yard to the London and South Western Railway, who conveniently provided a siding so that London refuse could be brought down and burned and the ashes used in making a cheaper type of brick. The level crossing where the railway crosses Little Heath Lane is now known as Cooks Crossing. Cook's directorship of the railway had no doubt helped in getting the line to pass through his land.

By all accounts, Cook's 'brickies' and their families were well cared for and received Christmas presents of brandy, poultry and coal. A free medical service was also provided as was 'the iron hut' which became a community centre and which was used as an evening games club for the men and, in the mornings, as an infant school for the children who were too young to walk to Cobham or Oxshott schools. In the afternoons, the local women met there for a chat, passing their time in sewing and knitting and, on Sunday afternoons, it was used for church services.

Cook died at Knowle Hill in 1904 aged 81 and was buried in the family vault at Cheshunt. His kindness and generosity were evidenced by his will, in which the sale proceeds of the Knowle Hill estate — up to £30,000 — were left to the Peabody Donation Fund. Other gifts were to hospitals and charitable organisations. Many of the longer-serving employees received annuities of up to £30.

Cook's brickyard was later taken over by W.E. Benton, who found the site had considerable drainage problems. Canadian soldiers occupied it during the two world wars, the brickyard was finally closed in 1960 and a modern estate has now been built around the water-filled clay pit.

The manufacture of motor cars is one of Cobham's more unlikely industries. Between 1918 and 1932 The Cottage on the Fairmile was the home of Invicta Cars, founded by Noel Macklin. When the business was sold off in 1933, Macklin started a new company called Fairmile Engineering, which imported chassis from the USA onto which were built their own cars. Reid Railton of 'Bluebird' and Napier Railton of land-speed record fame became a consultant, and lent his name to a new car, which became the fastest and most successful of the British Straight-Eights of the thirties, some 1,400 being produced and sold, of which a large number survive to this day. 'He shall have chariots easier than air' was the slogan adopted to introduce the Railton which *Autocar* summed up as 'ten years ahead of its time'.

The sales of cars dropped off in the late 1930s and Railton cars were sold to American Hudson Motors in 1939. It was then decided to concentrate on the war effort and Fairmile Engineering Company made a fast patrol boat of a type that could be produced in quantity. The 'Fairmile' motor gun boat saw extensive wartime service and earned Macklin a knighthood in 1946.

After the war, Fairmile Engineering was taken over by the Ministry of Defence. In recognition of the secret work done here the Admiralty presented Cobham with a ship's bell from HMS *Cobham* and this now hangs in the Borough Council's offices.

Private schooling has been an important feature of Cobham for many years and is now represented by the American Community School at Heywood, Feltonfleet School on the Byfleet

Road and Reeds School in Sandy Lane. Other private schools can be found in Stoke D'Abernon and Oxshott.

Reed's is worthy of inclusion in any account of Cobham, particularly because of its many famous old boys. The original school, formerly known as Sandroyd, was started in 1890 by Rev Wellesley-Wesley, Vicar of Hatchford, in a house in Green Lane. One of his pupils was Prince Charles of Saxe-Coburg-Gotta. In 1905 a new school was built on the present site in Sandy Lane. Former pupils included Randolph Churchill, Anthony Eden, Prince Peter of Yugoslavia, Prince Michael of Rumania and King Hussain of Jordan. The Cobham school was evacuated to Wiltshire during the Second World War and in 1946 Reed's School moved here from Watford.

In the late 1930s A. L. Tozer started selling vegetable seeds from his home in Cobham to market gardeners in the home counties. In 1944 Mr Tozer and Dr C. D. R. Dawson formed A. L. Tozer Ltd and two years later purchased Pyports. The company has developed many new varieties of vegetables including a lettuce called Cobham Green. In 1963 the Dawson family took over.

Holden's Forge in Cobham High Street. INSET: Trade card of Harvey Lee, Street Cobham.

ABOVE LEFT: Old House in Cobham High Street by E. Hassell 1827, demolished for RIGHT: the former Gammons building; CENTRE LEFT: Eldred Ledger, watch and clock maker in RIGHT: Church Street, c1890, looking towards the junction with High Street. BELOW LEFT: George Brown's original shop in the High Street, now 'Katie James', and RIGHT: his new shop, c1905.

Cobham,
Surrey
March 7th 1908

Miss F. Emery was in my Employ for about six years. I have found her honest & trustworthy & of good business qualities

Leaving on her own account to better herself

R.F. Lucas

ABOVE: Christmas's Timber Yard in Between Street, now Waitrose Supermarket, and BELOW: reference for Miss F. Emery from R. F. Lucas of Lucas's Stores, Street Cobham, in 1908.

ESHER 270

Tel.: ~~OXSHOTT 36~~

DIRECTORS:
W. E. BENTON (Chairman).
N. M. BENTON.
W. A. COLLINS.

# OXSHOTT BRICK WORKS LTD.

"PERRAN," ~~COBHAM, SURREY~~
BEACONSFIELD ROAD, Nov. 19th. 1940
CLAYGATE, SURREY. ....................193=

Dear Sirs,

As the Military Authorities have
requisitioned our Works our Office and records
have been removed to:-

"PERRAN," BEACONSFIELD ROAD, CLAYGATE, SURREY,
to which all correspondence should be addressed
until further notice.

Yours faithfully,
For OXSHOTT BRICK WORKS LTD.,

OPPOSITE ABOVE: Card from Oxshott Brick Works Ltd, 1940; CENTRE
LEFT: Henry Clements, hairdresser and wigmaker and RIGHT: T.
Andrews, decorator and sign writer, Post Boys Row; BELOW: West's Stores,
River Hill, c1930; 'Ye Olde Cottage Rooms' is now 'La Capana'. LEFT:
Harvey Bros Stores on the corner of Anyards Road and Portsmouth Road;
RIGHT: Dear & West — Boot Makers — River Hill. BELOW: Norwood
Farm Dairy, c1916.

## MRS. ARNOLD'S "MOTHERS' MEETING."

The women who attend the pleasant afternoon weekly meetings, in which Mrs. Arnold has for some years shown so great an interest, and which during this winter have been held in the Parish Nurse's Cottage, were, with their children, entertained by Mrs. Arnold, on Wednesday, December 30, to a sumptuous Tea, at the Workmen's Hall. The party assembled at 4 P.M., and were soon seated at the two long tables prepared for the mothers and children respectively. Grace was said by the Vicar; and the kind hostess, and Miss Arnold, Mrs. Richard Arnold, and numerous willing assistants, were most assiduous in their attendance on the guests, who lost no time in doing justice to the ample fare provided. Sweets and crackers were afterwards distributed; and the singing of some hymns, and instrumental music by Miss Arnold, brought a much-enjoyed treat to a close.

ABOVE LEFT: Matthew Arnold, from the portrait by G.F. Watts; RIGHT: Painshill Cottage shortly before demolition in 1963.
CENTRE LEFT: Mrs Arnold's Mothers' Meeting from the Parish Magazine 1886, and RIGHT: Mrs Humphrey Ward, novelist and niece of Matthew Arnold, and BELOW: the view from Leigh Hill around the turn of the century.

136

# Matthew Arnold

Of all the great and famous personalities who have visited Cobham or who have passed through along the old Portsmouth Road, only a few ever made their homes in the village. Of these the most distinguished was Matthew Arnold, who lived at Pains Hill Cottage between 1873 and 1888.

Arnold the poet, critic, philosopher and school inspector was the son of the famous Dr Thomas Arnold of Rugby School who was immortalised in *Tom Brown's School Days* by Thomas Hughes. The Arnold family had lived in Laleham, Middlesex, during Matthew's childhood. After leaving the district, Matthew later took up residence in Harrow, where his sons were at school, and there they met Charles John Leaf, a city merchant, whose sons were also at the school. The two families became close friends and when Leaf purchased the Painshill estate at Cobham, the Arnolds moved with them.

The Arnold's home had been part of the Painshill estate for at least a hundred years when they took up residence. In an 1831 Sales Catalogue the cottage was described in fashionable taste as 'an elegant cottage ornee'. A 1904 Sales Catalogue records that it had a Drawing Room, Dining Room and Morning Room, together with the usual offices and eight bedrooms. Sadly, the cottage was demolished in 1964 and its site is now occupied by a small housing estate named Matthew Arnold Close.

Matthew Arnold moved to Cobham with his wife Fanny Lucy, his son, two daughters and an assortment of animals. A strongly built man with dark hair and dark bushy side whiskers and sporting a monocle he must soon have become a familiar figure. He loved the cottage and the surrounding countryside and, in December 1873, he wrote to Lady de Rothschild:

'The cottage we have got there is called Pains Hill Cottage . . . The country is beautiful — more beautiful even than the Chilterns, because it has heather and pines, while the trees of other kinds, in the valley of the Mole, where we are, are really magnificent. And St. George's Hill and wood of I know not how many acres, practically quite open, is a continual pleasure. We are planting and improving about our cottage as if it were our own and we had a hundred years to live there; its great merit is that it must have had one hundred years of life already, and is surrounded by great old trees — not the raw sort of villa one generally has to take if one wants a small house near London'.

There was a pleasant view from the house south-westwards to Painshill with its great cedars and beautiful landscaped park. Arnold was often at Painshill House to dine with the Leafs and to play billiards, and his published letters contain many references to his local social life. The Arnolds used Painshill Park as their own and a favourite sport was skating on the lake during the winter months.

'On Christmas Day (1886) we skated at Pains Hill — beautiful ice.'
'The Pains Hill lake and woods were a sight.'

Walking and riding were the poet's other two great pleasures and he would often walk 'the Burwood round' with his dogs, through the grounds of his neighbour the Countess of Ellesmere.

The family pets were an important feature of life in the Arnold household. The death of his pony Lola at Cobham in 1886 caused him much sadness. Max and Geist were two of 'the dear dear dogs'. When Geist died in 1880 Arnold wrote the poem *Geist's Grave* and Kaiser was another dog immortalised in verse. In addition to various cats, another member of the household was his daughter's canary, Matthias. The bird died in 1882 and is remembered in the poem *Poor Matthias*.

With the opening of the local railway station in 1885, Arnold found it 'a pleasant walk to Cobham station for the 5.7 train'. On another occasion he records having walked with friends 'as far as Fair Mile, where we left them and came home by Leigh Hill. The distant hills were beautiful'.

Gardening was another pleasure that Matthew enjoyed with Fanny Lucy. In 1879 they are recorded as transplanting some holly and laurel bushes and, four years later, they were planting cypresses and thuyas. In October 1885 they spent a whole morning up ladders gathering their crop of pears and walnuts.

Arnold was not only a poet but also one of the greatest minds of his age. His writing and lecturing on society and religion have been called prophetic and another author has called him 'the Father of English Modernism'. His books on religion lead the reader to consider what is, and what is not, essential to a Christian faith. A.L. Rowse has written that 'of all Victorian writers Matthew Arnold was the one who left the most abiding mark upon English society'. Despite Arnold's unorthodox personal religious beliefs, both he and his family were regular attenders at the parish church. While at Cobham, he published a number of his most important works including *God and the Bible* and *Last Essays on Church and State*.

At Cobham, the Arnold family became thoroughly involved in the life of the local community and subscribed to local charities such as the Clothing Club, the Coal Club and the School Trust. The poet himself subscribed to the new village hall and his wife was involved in the many ladies' organisations of the parish. Fanny Lucy also had her own private charities and each December she would ascertain which families had no money to buy a Christmas dinner, and would then both make and deliver it to them herself. On at least two occasions, Matthew and his wife entertained village mothers and their children to a Christmas tea at the Working Men's Hall in Street Cobham and, in 1887, thirty women and eight children were entertained at Pains Hill Cottage and the parish magazine records how, on that occasion the chief attraction was the infant grand-daughter of the house.

Matthew's daughter, Lucy, had married Frederick Whittridge, a wealthy American whom they had met in New York, in December 1884 and this was one of the chief events of the Cobham social calendar. Local builders erected arches and other decorations along the route from the bride's home to the parish church and many houses were decorated for the occasion. Celebrities came down from London and people stood on the pews to see better and chatter about them — behaviour for which they were afterwards reprimanded by the vicar. In addition to that of Arnold himself, the signatures on the marriage registers include those of W.E. Forster, Henry James, A.J. Mundella MP, and Charles Combe.

Although Arnold had once described himself as the hermit of the Mole, his life at Cobham was not the life of a recluse. Many friends enjoyed the warmth of the family's hospitality, including his niece, the writer, Mrs Humphrey Ward, who later recalled 'the modest Cobham cottage . . . the garden beside the Mole where every bush and flower bed had its history; and that little study-dressing room where some of the best work in nineteenth century letters was done'.

Other friends in the area included the Buxtons of Foxwarren, the Evelyns of Wotton, near Dorking, the Deacons of Hatchford and the Maxses of Effingham. On one occasion the Maxses dinned at Pains Hill Cottage and there met Charles Leaf's son Walter, a distinguished classical scholar, and his friend, the scholar and writer Andrew Lang.

In 1885 Matthew Arnold received warning signs of the illness that was to lead to his death. He wrote of 'horrid pains across my chest' and realised that, like his father and grandfather, he had *angina pectoris.* He cut back his outdoor pursuits by giving up tennis and reducing his skating at Painshill. In a letter he writes 'imagine my having to stop half a dozen times in going up Pains Hill!'.

In April 1888 Matthew and Fanny Lucy left Cobham for Liverpool to meet their daughter and her family, returning from America. While in that city, Matthew Arnold died suddenly of heart failure on his way to meet the ship. His body was brought back to Cobham, whence it was taken to be buried near other family graves at Laleham.

For many years after his death Arnold's study was kept as he left it and Mrs Humphrey Ward recalled 'his coat hanging behind the door, his slippers beside the chair, the last letters he had received, and all the small and simple equipment of his writing table ready to hand'. Fanny Lucy remained at Pains Hill Cottage until her death in June 1901.

A small brass plate in St Andrew's Church to the memory of Arnold and his wife was placed there by the Ellesmere family of Burwood.

ABOVE: Painshill, c1905; BELOW: the view to Painshill House from the meadow behind Arnold's house, c1905.

ABOVE LEFT: South Eastern Gas Board showrooms (Holly Lodge), demolished 1966; RIGHT: Home Counties Dairies, demolished 1964; CENTRE LEFT: Kippins Ltd, demolished 1966; RIGHT: Ham Cottage, demolished in the 1960s, all in High Street; BELOW LEFT: cottages on River Hill, demolished for road widening in the 1960s, and RIGHT: Cedar House, preserved by the National Trust.

# Cobham Today

The past twenty years have seen enormous changes in Cobham as old buildings have been replaced by new roads and modern shops. Regrettably, a good deal of the old village was lost forever during the speculative days of the 1960s, which transformed so many of our old towns and villages. Cobham High Street suffered the most, losing the former Gas Showrooms — a fine eighteenth century building which commanded an important central site — and the former Home Counties Dairy building, built in the early years of this century in the style of a Swiss chalet.

The cottages on River Hill, dating from the eighteenth century and earlier, were demolished for road widening and, at the other end of the High Street, the former doctor's house and surgery were replaced by Oakdene Parade.

At first few voices were raised in protest at this destruction of our past but, as 'Progress' progressed, it was generally realised that before long Cobham would become yet another faceless suburban town.

The Cobham Conservation Group was formed in 1973 after the Cobham Residents Association had been instrumental in the creation of the town's first Conservation Area, which took in Church Street and the riverside. Since then, two further conservation areas have been created to include most of Downside and the Tilt. It is hoped that one day a bridge will be built over the Mole at Ash Ford, thus effectively linking the three areas together, and providing a circular walk around the most attractive parts of Cobham.

The former Old Cottage Restaurant (built around a fifteenth century hall house) was saved from threatened demolition and is now a successful Italian restaurant. Cobham Mill, owned by Surrey County Council, has been leased to a tenant who is to restore the building to working order and thus preserve an important Cobham landmark. Work is well in hand on the restoration of the landscape park at Painshill, which will not only become a great tourist attraction when the work is complete, but which will also furnish Cobham with a much needed 'breathing space' on the perimeter of the town.

Cobham still has plenty to show of its past, most notably in the conservation areas. Cedar House, a property of the National Trust, stands overlooking the river and is essentially a fifteenth century building encased in eighteenth century and later additions. The fine ornamental wrought iron gates came from the home of the playwright Sheridan at Eltham.

Nearby is the Old Mill House, traditional home of Cobham's millers. The smoke-blackened rafters of the house show that it began as a mediaeval open hall house. The house was extended and the smoke was contained, first in a smoke bay at one end and later in a central chimney stack. The front of the house has a long applied eighteenth century brick facade now rendered over. At the rear of the house is the eighteenth century barn with pigeon boxes and huge doors which, when opened, created a drying cross wind.

Next to the Old Mill House is Ham Manor, probably Cobham's finest period building and one of the best early eighteenth century houses in Surrey. Built about 1740, it has a mansard roof, a symmetrical facade and a central Tuscan Doric doorcase. It has many intersting original features including a leather studded door and wig cupboard or powder room.

In Church Street there is Church Stile House, a rare example in Surrey of a seventeenth century half timbered building with a double overhang. The red brick wing at the back is late 17th century. However, an older house existed on the site and in the thirteenth century Alan, Abbot of Chertsey bought it for 20s of silver. It was at that time let to Henry, curate of Cobham. In 1614 a brewer called Roger Bellow gave the house to the Churchwardens of Clerkenwell on condition that 20s yearly out of the rent be distributed to the poor on Good Friday. It later served as a house of rest for gentlewomen and a school for crippled children. It is now a private residence.

Across the road is Overbye, the core of which is at least 250 years old. This was once the home of Leonard Martin the architect who restored Church Stile House and designed Sandroyd (now Reed's) School.

Completing the group around the church is Pyports. Here a deceiving Georgian facade and Victorian additions hide a much earlier building. The house takes its name from the family who lived here. A William Le Pypard is recorded in 1332. In the eighteenth century it was the home of the Freeland family and in 1798 John Freeland insured 'his new dwellinghouse only near the church' for £900.

Lime House is a pleasing early eighteenth century building. At one time the house was split, the east wing being called Somers, while the main part of the house was called Christmas. Somers was used at various times by bakers and butchers.

Street Cobham contains a number of good period buildings including the White Lion where, yet again, an eighteenth century brick facade hides a much older building. (It is now the Vermont Exchange). Messrs Shoosmith and Lee, who have their original forge still standing behind their shop premises on the Portsmouth Road, can rightly claim to be Cobham's oldest surviving local business having started in the 1820s. Next to their shop are a pair of fine eighteenth century houses whose appearance has been slightly marred by the insertion of modern bow windows.

At the other end of Cobham, on the Tilt, are a variety of houses of various periods, including Korea Cottages, a good example of late nineteenth century estate cottages that have managed to retain their uniform brick facades. Nos 9 and 10 Korea Cottages are of an earlier date and probably represent the last of the old Workhouse cottages.

A little further along is Ashford Farm House. *The Place Names of Surrey* refers to 'the home of John de Ashford' in 1332 although the existing building is mostly 15th century. It is a three bay timber framed hall house with a brickwork facade that probably dates from Regency times and which is decorated with brick pilasters.

Important buildings of a more recent date are Cobham Park on the Downside Road, designed by E.M. Barry, and Benfleet Hall in Green Lane, designed by William Morris's colleague, Philip Webb.

The need for new homes, shops and roads has put considerable pressure on Cobham. However it has managed to retain much of its identity, helped by the surrounding commons and farm land, which separate it from adjoining towns.

A new Day Centre for the retired has added to local amenities and it is hoped that a new Village Centre will follow shortly.

While buildings and environments are essential in the preservation of our heritage, it is the local people who will make a community what it is, and it is ultimately they who can ensure the continued survival of the character of the place. Cobham is fortunate in having a strong core of people who feel a commitment to the town, and who have striven to maintain and enhance both its character and environment, as well as the general quality of life in this area. To those people we owe a great debt. It is often commented that, while Cobham has outgrown the strict definition of a village, enough of the 'village' atmosphere has survived to make it a very pleasant place in which to live.

LEFT: Anyards Road, Cobham, c1925. Most of the buildings on the right have been replaced by modern shops. The building in the middle distance was the studio of Hugh West the Cobham photographer and is now the site of a supermarket. RIGHT: Ham Manor from the drawing by John L. Baker; BELOW: Church Stile House — one of Cobham's finest old buildings.

LEFT: Tilt Road, Cobham, c1915 — the Tilt is now one of Cobham's three conservation areas — and CENTRE: Korea Cottages, Tilt Road, also c1915. RIGHT: A scene in the garden of Ham Manor, c1890. The roofs of the buildings on River Hill can be seen in the background. BELOW: the Chapel and Old Pump at Downside, now a conservation area.

144

ABOVE LEFT: Cobham High Street — a tranquil scene from the early years of this century. The large tree on the left was in the garden of Holly Lodge and is now the site of Barclays Bank. The Post Office and shops on the right still stand; RIGHT: Cobham at War — the Triumphal Arch erected at the junction of Between Streets and High Street at the end of the first World War; CENTRE: a bomb crater in Stoke Road, near Oxshott Way, and Canadian soldiers stationed in Cobham during the second World War; BELOW: Leg Of Mutton Field, a rural scene from the turn of the century;

ABOVE: Cobham High Street, c1870; BELOW: the same view today.

# Select Bibliography & Further Reading

Albert, William *The Turnpike Road System in England 1663-1840* C.U.P. (1972)

Allison, William *My Kingdom for a Horse* Grant Richards Ltd 1919

Alsop, James *Gerrard Winstanley's Later Life* Past & Present No 82 (1979)

Arnold, Matthew *Letters 1848-1888* (2 vols) Macmillan & Co (1895)

Aubrey, John *History of Surrey (1718-19)* Kohler & Coombes (1975)

Bates, Alan *Virginia Woolf — A Biography* The Hogarth Press (1972)

Brayley, W.E. *History of Surrey*

Brockway, Fenner *Britain's First Socialists* Quartet (1980)

Chambers, R. *The Strict Baptist Chapels of England: Surrey and Hants*

Cleal, Edward E. *The Story of Congregationalism in Surrey* (1908)

Cobham Conservation Group *Cobham: A Short History & Guide to the Conservation Areas* (1980)

Copeland, John *Roads and their Traffic 1750-1850* David & Charles (1968)

Crooks, Rev F.W. *The Parish Church of St Andrew, Cobham* (1960)

Defoe, Daniel *A Tour Through The Whole Island of Great Britain* (1724 and 1742)

*Dictionary of National Biography*

Earle, Mrs T. *Pot-Pourri from a Surrey Garden; More Pot-Pourri from a Surrey Garden; A Third Pot-Pourri*

Earle, Mrs T. and Miss E. Case *Pot-Pourri Mixed By Two*

Ellis, S.M. *George Meredith* Grant Richards Ltd (1920)

Fairfax Lucy, Alice *The Lucys of Charlecote*

Gaunt, William *The Pre-Raphaelite Tragedy* Sphere Books Ltd (1975)

Greenwood, George *Elmbridge Water Mills* (1980)

Haynes, Richard *Esher Quakers* (1971)

Hill, Christopher *The World Turned Upside Down* Pelican; *Winstanley: The Law of Freedom and Other Writings; The Religion of Gerrard Winstanley* Past & Present (1978)

Hardy, F.E. *The Life of Thomas Hardy 1840-1928* Macmillan

Huntington, William *The Bank of Faith* (Centenary Edition) (1913)

Horne, Pamela *The Rural World 1780-1850* Hutchinson (1980)

Hoskins, W.G. *The Making of the English Landscape* Pelican

Hodges, Alison *Painshill Park* Garden History Society Journal, Vol II No 2, Vol III No 1, Vol III No 2. (The first of these articles contains a full Bibliography of Painshill)

Janes, Hurford *The Red Barrel — A History of Watney Mann* John Murray (1963)

Langham-Carter, R.R. *Pains Hill Cottage — Matthew Arnold's Surrey Home* Surrey Archaeological Society Collection Vol 67; *The Arnolds at Painshill Cottage* Surrey Archaeological Society Collections Vol 69

Malcolm, J. *Modern Husbandry of Surrey* (3 Vols) (1805)

Manning and Bray *History of Surrey* (1804-1814)

Millward and Robinson *Landscapes of Britain Series: Thames and the Weald* Macmillan

Molesworth, Caroline *The Cobham Journals*

Moorman, Mary *William Wordsworth* Oxford

Morris, John (Ed) *History from the Sources: Domesday Book: Surrey* Phillimore

Nairn and Pevsner *The Buildings of England: Surrey* Penguin

Orr, J. Edwin *Second Evangelical Awakening in Britain* Marshall Morgan and Scott (1949)

Pocock, W.W. *A History of Wesleyan Methodism in Some of the Southern Counties of England* (1885)

Pepys, Samuel *Dairy*

Postan, M.M. *The Medieval Economy and Society* Pelican (1975)

Pulford, J.S.L. *The First Kingston Quakers* (1973)

Sambrook, James *Painshill Park in the 1760s* Garden History Society Journal Vol VIII No 1

Stenton, D.M. *English Society in the Early Middle Ages* Pelican (1951)

Sheppard Frere, MA, FSA *Report on the Roman Bath House at Chatley* Surrey Archaeological Society Collections Vol 50

Smith, Reginald A. *Romano-British Remains at Cobham* Surrey Archaeological Society Collections Vols 21 and 22

Stevenson, W. *Agriculture of Surrey* (1813)

Taylor, D.C. *Painshill Park* Esher News (1964 and 1971); *Methodism in Cobham* Esher News (1970); *When Cobham Nearly had a Railway* Esher News (1970); *Looking Back at Cobham* Esher News (1972); *Cobham Park Logica* (1981); *Cobham Brewery — A Short History* (1981); *Gerrard Winstanley in Elmbridge* Elmbridge Borough Council (1982); *The Leafs of Painshill* Esher District Local History Society Newsletter No 54

Tye, Walter *The Life Story of John Earley Cook* Esher News (1970); *The Fairmile Since the Nineties* Esher News (1969)

Trevor, Meriol *The Arnolds* The Bodley Head (1973)

*The Place Names of Surrey* English Place Name Society Vol XI

Walker, T.E.C. *Cobham: Manorial History* Surrey Archaeological Society Collection Vol 58; *The Chase of Hampton Court* Surrey Archaeological Society Collection Vol 62; *Cobham Incumbents and Curates* Surrey Archaeological Society Collection Vol 71; *The Diary of Admiral Graham Moore* Surrey Archaeological Society Collection Vol 60; *Cobham Spas* Esher District Local History Society Newsletter No 34

Ward, Mrs Humphrey *A Writers Recollections*

Wesley, John *Journals* Epworth Press

Whitworth, Rex *Lord Ligonier*

Wright, Thomas *The Life of William Huntington S.S.* Farncombe & Son (1909)

Wilson, Geoffrey *The Old Telegraphs* Philimore & Co (1976)

*Victoria County History of Surrey*

*The Surrey Record Society have published a number of volumes with material which relate to Cobham. The volumes concerning the Chertsey Cartulary and the Surrey Quarter Sessions have been consulted for this work, as have the Calendar of Assize Records — Surrey Indictments for the reigns of Elizabeth I and James I which have been published by HMSO.*

*The chief source for unpublished material relating to the history of Cobham is the Surrey Record Office at both Kingston and Guildford. Here are deposited many of the records of both the manor and parish. Other material can be consulted in the Public Record Office whilst certain parish records are still retained by St Andrew's Church.*

*Excavated material and other items relating to Cobham can be seen in the museums at Guildford and Weybridge.*

# AUTHOR'S NOTE

*The Book of Cobham* first appeared in 1982 and has been out of print for some while. This fourth impression is in response to continuing demand. Since first publication, there have been new discoveries concerning Cobham's history and changes in the town. Cobham Mill has been restored and opened to the public, as has the Semaphore Tower on Chatley Heath. Restoration work at Painshill Park makes good progress and a full opening is expected soon. The author hopes to produce a new book dealing with more recent discoveries concerning Cobham's past. In the meantime it is felt that a further edition of this book, which paints a broad picture of the development of Cobham, could appear without the need for major changes or additions.

David Taylor
*January 1995.*

ENDPAPERS: Front: John Speede's Map of Surrey, 1610; Back: Part of John Rocque's Map of Surrey, c1760.

Darnford Bridge

Tunnensley Farm

Woodham

Motal Farm

Broock Land

Newham Locks & Bridge

Woodham Heath

Ham How

Common

Shire Pond

Purford

Common Nanyhelet River

Heath

Heath

Byfleet

Byfleet Bridge

Byfleet

By·fleet

Steel Mills

Burchet Far

Sec

Wistley

Purford Locks

Purford Green

Wistley Pond

Red Hill

und Bridge Farm

Purford

Purford Green

Wistley

Common

Ockham Park

Newark Abby

Purford Lodge

Newark Mill

Walsom Warren

23 M

Breath Hill

Purford Court

Walsom Meadow

28 M

Home Wood Farm

Ripley

Ockham Heath

Hide Farm

Green

Ripley

Lord Kings

Ockham

Breach Field

Relcote

Green

D · R

Grove Heath

Soils Hill Farm

Haynes Heath

E · D

26 M

Brick Kiln

Hanare Hill

Ride Farm

Black Heath Land